Women
of the
Twelfth Century

WITHDRAWN

Women
of the
Twelfth Century

Volume Two:
Remembering the Dead

Georges Duby

Translated by Jean Birrell

The University of Chicago Press

GEORGES DUBY was a member of the Académie Française, and taught for many years at the Collège de France. Of his many books, five have been published in translation by the University of Chicago Press: *The Three Orders; The Age of the Cathedrals; The Knight, the Lady, and the Priest; History Continues;* and *Love and Marriage in the Middle Ages.* The University of Chicago Press and Polity Press are publishing *Women of the Twelfth Century,* in three volumes.

The University of Chicago Press, Chicago 60637

Polity Press, Cambridge CB2 1UR, UK

First published in French as *Dames du XIIe Siècle, II: Le souvenir des aïeules* © Éditions Gallimard, 1995.

First published in English in 1997 by the University of Chicago Press and by Polity Press in association with Blackwell Publishers Ltd.

Published with the assistance of the French Ministry of Culture.

Printed in Great Britain

06 05 04 03 02 01 00 99 98 97 1 2 3 4 5 6

Library of Congress Cataloging-in-Publication Data

Duby, Georges.
  [Dames du XIIème siècle. English]
  Women of the twelfth century / Georges Duby : translated by Jean Birrell.
    p. cm.
  Contents: v. 1. Eleanor of Aquitaine and six others.
  ISBN 0–226–16776–0 (cloth : v. 1 : alk. paper).—ISBN 0–226–16780–1 (pbk. : v. 1 : alk. paper)
    1. Women—France—History—Middle Ages, 500–1500. 2. Women —France—Biography. I. Title.
HQ1147.F7D813 1997
305.4′ 0944′ 0902—DC21   97–14198
                                                          CIP

ISBN: 0–226–16783–6 (Vol. 2, cloth)
ISBN: 0–226–16784–4 (Vol. 2, ppbk)

This book is printed on acid-free paper.

Contents

Introduction   1

Part I
Serving the Dead   3

1 *The Dead within the House*   5
2 *Women and the Dead*   10
3 *Writing about the Dead*   16
4 *Remembering Women*   29

Part II
Wives and Concubines   41

1 *The Genealogy of a Eulogy*   43
2 *The Trouble with Women*   51
3 *Wives*   61
4 *Mistresses*   69
5 *Arlette*   80

Part III
The Power of Women   89

1 *The Context*   93
2 *The Witness*   110
3 *Mother Goddesses*   118
4 *The Couple*   127
5 *Widows*   140

  Genealogies   150

Introduction

In the twelfth century, the nobility honoured its dead. It lavished most attention on the dead men of the family, but the women were not forgotten. Their names were repeated and their virtues and the role they had played in the history of the lineage were recalled. A time came when it was decided to put into writing these words commemorating the ancestors. A specific literary genre was born, which flourished throughout the northern half of France in the second half of the twelfth century. By chance, a few of these writings have been preserved: those composed in honour of the dukes of Normandy, the counts of Flanders, the counts of Anjou and the sires of Amboise, the counts of Guînes and the lords of Ardres. I have them before me now. They tell us a great deal about what life was like in those great houses, and no documents show more clearly, in what was remembered and what forgotten, how the knights and the priests thought about the women of their blood. Consequently, a few female figures emerge from obscurity. They are less clear than the symbolic figures of the princesses, female saints and heroines of popular romances that I discussed in my previous volume. They are sufficiently distinct, nevertheless, to shed a little light on what I am attempting to discover: the condition of women and how the wives of lords lived in the twelfth century.

Part I

Serving the Dead

1

The Dead within the House

In the twelfth century, no one doubted that the dead were
alive. It might not be clear where, but they lived. Their
presence was felt in a number of ways and care was taken
to propitiate them. Because, beyond the invisible barrier they
had crossed, in their mysterious abode, where time passed at
the same rate as here below, most of them suffered. They
were in pain, which made them aggressive, vindictive and
wicked. The dead were frightening.

Until they had been laid in the ground, people feared them.
Henry Plantagenet liked to hear the story of the adventures
of Richard I, duke of Normandy, the great-great-grandfather
of his grandfather. God apart, this prince feared nothing.
Like all knights, he ceaselessly roamed the countryside, but
he liked also to wander at night, braving danger, flouting the
evil forces lurking in the shadows, which most people
guarded against by shutting themselves up inside their
houses. One night, having gone out alone to hunt, he found
himself before the door of a chapel. As was his custom, he
went in to say a short prayer. Approaching the altar, he
passed without flinching an open and occupied coffin. He
heard it move behind his back. Twice, he shouted: 'Lie down,
will you!' adding, 'You're the very devil.' He completed his
prayer, crossed himself, commended his soul to God, then
turned round to leave. At this point he saw the corpse

towering before him, broad, tall, arm outstretched; it looked to him like a devil. He drew his sword and felled this creature barring his way. He cut it through the middle, left, then, unperturbed, retraced his steps in order to look for a glove he had forgotten. Nevertheless, warned by this encounter, he ordered that the dead should no longer be left alone at night before they were buried, shut up in a sarcophagus.

Even after they had been buried, people were wary of the dead, because they sometimes returned. They did so to warn, or to deliver a message from heaven or, more often, to seek help from their family or take revenge on them for neglecting them. They spoke and they also listened. A dialogue was sometimes struck up. In 1325 – which was some two hundred years after the story of Richard I's adventures had been put into writing, during which time rational thought had, after all, made some progress – John Gobi, a Dominican, reported to the Avignon pope, John XXII, what he had learned from a dead man; this was a burgess of Alès who had died some weeks earlier but who was returning home from time to time and upsetting and harassing his widow. John had asked the mayor of the town to have the house surrounded by two hundred armed men, all duly confessed, so as to prevent any subterfuge. Accompanied by a master of theology, the philosophy teacher from his convent and a notary, he went to the house and, with great persistence, compelled the dead man to answer all the questions he had prepared. He eventually got him to say that there were in fact two purgatories, one where all the souls congregated during the day and which was situated at the centre of the earth, and another, a nocturnal one, where each dead person returned to the scene of his or her principal sin. The ancestors I am about to discuss were certainly less talkative. At any rate, nothing they said after their death is recorded in the histories which tell of their exploits. I am sure, however, of one thing: their descendants felt that they were close by. They were still part of the household.

The house or household – the *mesnie* and *masnade*, as they were called in the Romance dialects – constituted the most solid framework for all social relations in the twelfth century. These were thought and lived in a domestic form, whether in the case of relationships between the Christian and the Trinity, the Mother of God and the saints, or between the lord and his vassals, the master and his servants or the war leader and those who fought alongside him in battle. The society that we call feudal can be defined as an agglomeration of households, each under the authority of one, and only one, master. These houses, living organisms, sought to perpetuate their existence. It was therefore the primordial duty of the men who ruled them to procreate, to take a wife – the lady – and impregnate her. If they were loath to do this, their entourage compelled them. It was essential that, at the time of their death, they should be in a position to hand over the power which was slipping from their grasp into that of one of their sons, the eldest. In each noble house a dynasty was established and in all of them, procreation appeared as the chief act by which blood – that blood inherited from men and women no longer visible, whose mortal remains lay under the slab – passed from one body, which had reached maturity, into another body, which would grow and gain strength; in due course, that body would, in its turn, transmit the blood, sap of that tree whose roots were entrenched deep at the heart of the house that the ancestors had founded and enriched, and whose name was borne by most of their heirs. Furthermore, it was seen as essential that the trunk of the family tree should remain, down the ages, thick, straight and smooth, and that its vigour should not be sapped by an excessive proliferation of its branches. Heads of households felt obliged, consequently, to give a legitimate wife to only one of their sons, the one who would succeed them and, from this woman, produce his successor, who would also be unique.

The dynastic noble house was a strictly hierarchized body. All, in fact, was hierarchy in the world as it was then seen, each person dominated by others whom he must respect and serve, each person himself dominating others he must protect and cherish. This exchange of reverence and of love, this chain of mutual obligations, which the theologians of the age called by the word *caritas*, an abundant flow emanating from divine power and returning to its source, was seen as irrigating the whole of creation and conferring on it its necessary cohesion. The household was constructed according to this model and its members were distributed between three superimposed ranks. Two of these were visible and tangible: at the bottom, the children, obeying and serving; above, the father ruling over and nourishing them, his wife at his side and often also his brothers and sisters if they were unmarried. The diagram is simple. In each house, there was only one conjugal bed, only one place for licit procreation. Among the knights, many of whom died young, few heads of families saw the birth of their grandchildren; in any case, the latter – if their grandfather was still alive – came into the world in another house, that to which their grandfather had gone to bless his eldest son on the night of his marriage. That the household consisting of two generations constituted the basic structure is attested by the vocabulary of family relationships then in use: it was impoverished, its only precise terms distinguishing father and mother, brother and sister, son and daughter, husband and wife. Beyond this, to indicate cousinhood, there were only vague terms, which did not differentiate between paternal and maternal ancestry. This last feature is significant; the equivalence between the two branches in part explains why women occupied so important a position in the ancestral memory.

The third and top storey, meanwhile, was occupied by the dead parents. This dominant position was theirs by right; they had gone before and their successors profited from what they had left behind; it was only right that they should be honoured and served. In a society where all power relations took the form of an exchange of gifts and counter-gifts, this service (*obsequia*, 'obsequies': our way of referring to the funeral service still preserves the trace of this very ancient conception of the relations between the living and the dead), the duty to lavish attention on the ancestors, was to compensate for what each of their descendants had received: first, life, but also a patrimony, virtues and glory, all the advantages which they could enjoy on earth.

The dead lived. To serve them did not, therefore, consist

of making them live once again, but of maintaining their invisible presence within the household. They were present, first, through the name they had borne. The father of the family was expected to give this name to one of his children, who then appeared as a substitute, a reincarnation of the dead man, and felt himself obliged to imitate this grandfather or great-grandfather or great-great-grandfather, to prove himself as valiant and as virtuous as he had been, and to perform, if possible, the role he had once performed. Such a duty obliged him, obviously, to be familiar with the main facts regarding the eponymous ancestor, and assiduously to keep his image in mind. The dead, however, demanded more. To satisfy them, it was necessary also to turn to them periodically, to evoke them, to call them back. The ancestors were, in the precise meaning of the term, revenants; they resumed their place within the family circle each time that their surviving descendants gathered to recall their acts and their 'deeds'. To commemorate them solemnly on certain dates was an act that was strictly speaking vital because it served to revitalize the sap of the family tree. To repeat the names of the ancestors was, in effect, to revive the glory of their renown. And the renown of the ancestors constituted the strength of the lineage at a time when the status of a house, the rank assigned to it, its accumulated knowledge, in brief its nobility, was based on the memory of ancestral glories. What, indeed, was *nobilitas* if not the capacity to claim for oneself very distant and valorous ancestors?

2

Women and the Dead

Was the lady specially responsible within her own house for preserving the memory of the dead and for ensuring that their names did not fall into oblivion? This question is posed by a reading of Dhuoda, whose words, of all those spoken by a woman to survive from the Middle Ages, are the oldest we can hear directly. Dhuoda was a very great lady, wife of one of the highest dignitaries of the Frankish kingdom. In 841–3, she wrote a *Manual* for her son, who had just been removed from the gynaeceum in which he had spent his childhood, and placed by his father in the house, the 'great house', of King Charles the Bald, his kinsman. When he had reached the age of maturity, this boy would, in his turn, 'order his own house according to the proper hierarchies'. For the moment, the first duty laid down for him by his mother was 'reverence towards his father'. These words form the title of Book III of Dhuoda's *Manual*, the two previous books dealing with obligations towards God, who should be served first, and who was represented on earth by the father. So, house, paternity and submission to those who had gone before: the basis of the social order is here seen with great clarity, but so is the role of the lady, wife of the lord and teacher. 'You ought,' she says, 'whether he is present or absent, to fear your father [fear first, a reverential fear, the sort one felt

before images of God, or before reliquaries, or before the
dead], you ought to love him and be faithful to him in
everything ... I exhort you to love God first, then to love
and fear your father by saying to you that it is from him that
you derive your estate in the world.' The text is clear. Why
should one love and serve? In return for the gift received.
This son, William, owed, therefore, a similar allegiance to
that other father, the master of the house he had just entered,
who would provide for and educate him, the man 'whom
God and your father have chosen for you to serve in the full
vigour of your early youth'. He was to serve God, to serve
the two fathers and, to this end, pray regularly for them.
After that, he was to pray for the dead.

He should pray for all the dead, that innumerable throng
whose murmurings on the margins of the visible world
people believed they could hear, but in particular for the
'domestic' dead, the 'members of our family'. 'I, who am
going to die, command you to pray for all the dead, but
above all for those from whom you derive your origins' –
that is to say, blood and life. That life and that blood flowed
from two sources, paternal and maternal. Priority, however,
went 'to those of your father's relatives who left him their
possessions in lawful inheritance'. This sentence contains the
essence: the wealth that this eldest son will one day enjoy,
when his father has joined the ranks of the dead, will almost
all come to him from his father, hence from his father's
relatives; in his prayers, William is duty bound, consequently,
to recall their memory first, to name them first before God.
Further, the gift made to the dead by praying for them should
be in exact proportion to the gift received from each of them.
'In proportion to the goods they left [to your father], pray',
repeated Dhuoda, 'for those who held them before him and
for him to live to enjoy them for a long time [before handing
them over to you at his death] ... if something should be
surrendered to you earlier, pray as much as you can so that
the reward of the souls of those to whom it all belonged will
be increased.' The concern, it is clearly asserted, is of exactly
equal weight, in perfect equilibrium, and on this concern are
based two of the key structures of the ancestral memory: the

more they have bequeathed, the stronger is the remembrance of the dead; the memory of each one of them remains firmly attached to whichever of the various pieces of the patrimony, whichever house or piece of land or set of jewels they had formerly possessed. So William ought particularly to mention in his prayers the name of a paternal uncle, his godfather, who had 'adopted [him] as a son in Christ', because if he had lived, this man would have been a 'foster father', 'full of love', his third father, and most of all because, at the time of his death, treating his nephew and godson 'like his first-born son', he had already left all his possessions not to him but to his father, so that he would one day benefit. If the memory of the forefathers seems to be clearer and more firmly rooted than that of the female forebears, and if the names of women are less numerous than those of men in the texts written in the twelfth century to the glory of the ancestors, it is because the honours and the greater part of the property were usually transmitted at this period from father to son.

If the service of prayer and of commemoration was to be equitably divided between the ancestors, it was necessary to know their names. Dhuoda listed them carefully: 'You will find their names at the back of this book.' It was a list destined to lengthen as men and women, the ancestors, the legatees, would go, one after the other, to continue their existence elsewhere, in the hereafter. 'When someone of your lineage leaves this world, I ask you, if you survive them, to have their name transcribed with those of the persons recorded below.' He was to write, to put letters which would be forever legible on the parchment or on the stone and, in this way, to erect a memorial. The manual that Dhuoda wrote was such a memorial. So were the tombstones; on one face was engraved the name of the dead person they contained, and it was the duty of the descendants to make sure that the inscription was never obliterated.

Were there also images that were intended to preserve the memory of the ancestors? It is possible, but we simply do not know. The texts reveal that, for certain services, the monks of Cluny carried in procession the *imago* of St Peter, and that, from time to time, the true father of their brotherhood became once again, in this form, visibly present in their midst. If effigies of this sort, more fragile than the statue of St Peter, ever existed in the houses of princes, no trace of them survives from before the end of the eleventh century; there then appear, on the tombs of the greatest of them, sculpted or painted like that of the saints on church porches, the image of the dead man, lying full length on the catafalque, represented for eternity in the form that his body had assumed for the last time before the assembled, weeping household and before the crowd of poor who had come running to share in his last munificence.

However that may be, Dhuoda expected just one thing of this child who was quitting the nest: that he would not forget, later on, to write her name. 'When I too have ended my days, have my name transcribed among those of the dead. What I wish, what I beg with all my heart as if it were now, is that you have these verses securely inscribed on the stone of the tomb that will enclose my body, so that those who decipher the epitaph will pray to God worthily for me, who am unworthy.' In fact, her name appears twice in the poem she wrote to be engraved on her tomb, in the form of a cross, horizontally at the beginning of the second verse, and vertically as an acrostic of the eight initial letters.

This 'manual' is unique of its kind. Were other lists of ancestors dictated, which are now lost? Were they, too, the work of a wife, the mother of the heir presumptive, on the occasion of his entry into the world? It undoubtedly fell to men, as heads of household responsible for the patrimony, to take from it whatever was needed to reward appropriately the monks and priests who helped them to serve their dead well. However, there is some evidence – for example certain passages in the eulogies written about Matilda and Adelaide, wives and mothers of emperors – to suggest that it fell to women, responsible within the house, to see that the commemorations, when these took place within the home, were properly organized, and hence to preserve from oblivion the name of the deceased so that they could be evoked on the prescribed dates. It certainly fell to women, at all events, to lead the mourning at the funeral, to be the first to proclaim, as head of the female part of the household, the grief of the house.

It seems clear that there existed a privileged relationship between women and the deceased. We know almost nothing about the funerary rites at which ecclesiastics did not officiate. The little that we can deduce comes from the prelates who struggled throughout the ninth and tenth centuries, and who were still struggling in the year 1000, to root out the remnants of paganism, because they condemned, and consequently described, customs that were, in their eyes, execrable. From Hincmar, archbishop of Reims, from Regino of Prüm and from Burchard of Worms, we learn that, in north-eastern Gaul, in regions still savage, women were then being urged to abandon certain acts. They were instructed to cease from driving a stake into the ground through the corpses of women who had died in childbirth 'so that they did not return . . . to do serious harm to others', or through those of still-born babies or of infants buried without being baptized. They were to stop throwing a bucket of water under the stretcher when a dead body was being carried out of the house. They were no longer to impregnate with unguents the hands of warriors killed in battle. And priests who had participated in the funeral vigils should not, after the banquet, the libations and the songs which invited the dead person and, perhaps, with him, the ancestors he had gone to join in the other world, to return for a brief moment to the midst of the gathering, allow 'the dancers to perform before them disgusting acts, in the manner of the daughter of Herod'. Hincmar called these Salomes *tornatrices*, whirlers, and we may imagine them whirling themselves into a trance.

How much of such pagan activities survived in the twelfth century, we do not know. At least it was still regarded as essential that women should stay close to bodies that were awaiting burial. They should be seen to weep, to tear their clothes, to let down their hair, to pull it out by the handful and to scratch their cheeks, and they should proclaim their grief at the tops of their voices. When, at the beginning of the eleventh century, in his history of the dukes of Normandy, Dudo of Saint-Quentin gave an account of the funeral of a Viking chief who had died a century earlier, he described what he himself had seen. He shows the 'female sex' rushing out into the city streets to escort the catafalque, that is, women leaving the house, the private space in which they should properly remain confined, and fulfilling one, and I believe the only one, of their public functions: to make collective mourning visible and audible by their gestures and their terrible shrieking. When I open the chronicle of Galbert of Bruges, I read that, in 1127, immediately after the murder of Charles the Good, count of Flanders, it was women who 'watched over the body all that day and the following night, sitting all around, wailing and lamenting', and that when one of the murderers killed himself falling from the top of the tower in which he had taken refuge with his accomplices, it was again women, 'poor women . . . [who] carried him into a house and prepared his funeral'. Like the bodies of the new-born, the bodies of the dead were the responsibility of women. Their task was to wash and to dress them, as Mary Magdalen and her companions, walking towards the sepulchre of Jesus, were preparing to do on Easter morning. In the twelfth century, women's power – mysterious, dis-quieting and indubitable – was due principally to the fact that, as from the fertile earth, life came from their wombs and that when life was extinguished, it returned to them as to the welcoming earth. It seems that the two functions of femininity, maternal and funerary, made it the job of women to manage the 'obsequies', the services that the ancestors demanded of the living.

3

Writing about the Dead

C hristianization, however, had resulted in part of this task being given to the servants of God. By the seventh century, if not before, the dead were left to repose in places of prayer before being interred, and it became customary to bury them as close as possible to hallowed ground. This started the slow process by which cemeteries, previously set apart from the abode of the living, were brought into the immediate vicinity of the parish churches. The same impulse caused tombs to be clustered close to the great basilicas which were believed to receive the favours of heaven in the greatest abundance. Who, as death approached, did not wish to be carried, to await the Last Judgement, into the interior of these sumptuously decorated buildings, where one experienced, as soon as one crossed the threshold, what seemed like a foretaste of the splendours of paradise? Archaeologists, consequently, find sarcophagi and more modest tombs squeezed one on top of the other against the walls, as if jostling each other to force entry, but relegated nevertheless to the exterior, because for a long time only the bodies of saints and of those impregnated with sacred oil – kings and bishops – were allowed inside. The most powerful of the nobles demanded the same right. During the course of the tenth century, they appropriated it, along with other royal attributes, as part of that dispersal of the sovereign prerogative that we call feudalization.

Dudo of Saint-Quentin, from whom I quoted above, and whose superb work I will exploit at length below, described, as an eyewitness, the last moments of Duke Richard I of Normandy, who died in 996. A few lines earlier, Dudo had shown the duke evangelizing, in his own way, the still pagan Vikings, explaining to them what they should believe. Man, he told them, is made up of two elements, the flesh and the soul. Death separates one from the other, but the body is not completely destroyed; the soul, at the end of the world, will return and slip back into it, warmth will again penetrate the bones, and the blood will again flow, irrigate the flesh and 'reanimate' it. That is why, said Richard, Christians took such good care of sepulchres. He had been thinking about his own for some time. He had decided that his mortal remains should be transported to Fécamp. It was there that he had been baptized and that he had founded a monastery dedicated to the Trinity which towered over his own palace. It was there that he wanted to sleep his last sleep. He had given orders for his tomb, a sarcophagus of stone, to be prepared in advance. Every week, until he would lie there himself, it was to be filled with corn which was then to be distributed to the poor. When he fell ill, he was conveyed by litter from Bayeux to Fécamp. He got down, then removed his clothes, demonstrating by this act that he was changing his life. He put on the costume of the penitents, and barefoot, wearing a hair shirt, entered the church of the Trinity. Laying what finery he still retained on the altar, he received the viaticum. His half-brother, one of the sons of his mother, and his dearest friend, then asked him where the sarcophagus should be placed. Richard replied that his body, too stained with sin, was unworthy to be admitted into the sanctuary. It would lie at the door, under the gutter. Everyone was amazed. Such a gesture of humility was, in fact, rare. Princes of Richard's rank usually demanded that their sepulchre, like that of the Frankish kings in Saint-Denis, should be placed as near as possible to the relics of the saints, in the middle of a choir of men who would perpetually launch upwards to

heaven the invocation for the salvation of their soul. Like
Richard, they usually chose to be buried in a monastery.

The monastic communities seemed particularly well qualified to take charge of the dead. Vast and well-ordered
households, bands of brethren devoted to singing with one
voice, day and night, the glory of a God who, in return,
favoured them with his largess, they already magnificently
honoured one or more dead, the saints present in their
church in their effigy and in whatever was preserved of their
bodies. The liturgical splendour with which they surrounded
these remains culminated on the feast of these holy persons,
the anniversary of their death. The monks celebrated with
similar rites the office on behalf of other dead persons, their
brothers in religion and the more generous of their benefac-
tors, those men who had paid dearly to purchase entry into
the monastic 'society', and to be spiritually incorporated into
their 'fraternity'. Some of them, in the evening of their life,
brought their body at the same time as their offering, donning
in extremis the habit of St Benedict. Thus Richard I had
come to the church of the Trinity in Fécamp to renounce as
a monk the vanities of the world, and thus the count of
Anjou, Geoffrey Martel, 'the night that preceded his death,
put aside all concern with knighthood and with the affairs of
the world and became a monk in the monastery of Saint-
Nicholas of Angers'. In the eleventh century, the funerary
liturgies promised to these associates were organized according to a complex system. It reached perfection in the Cluniac
congregation, and was the reason for its spectacular success.

Like Dhuoda, the monks wrote. They kept books: *libri
memoriales*, 'aides-mémoire'. These catalogues listed those
who, on a given day, until the end of time, would be named
during the course of the offices, and in whose name, on that
day, the monks, having sung themselves hoarse on their
behalf, would be rewarded with an extra pittance and a
double ration of wine, the dead person then returning to
preside, invisibly, over their meal. Many names were preserved in this way in the monasteries. Should we therefore
conclude that the memory of the ancestors was kept more
faithfully by the monks than it was in their own home? Not

necessarily; the example of societies without writing shows that memory alone, if well exercised and constantly appealed to, as it used to be in the entourage of the kings of black Africa, and as it surely was in the aristocratic households of the twelfth century, is quite capable of keeping vividly in mind for centuries the most complicated of family trees. It could happen, nevertheless, that noble houses broke up or died out, or that the descendants neglected their duties. To turn to the monasteries might prove a safer bet. I agree with O. G. Oexle that monastic communities appeared better able, at this period, to 'manage social relations between the living and the dead . . . by the inscription and the recitation of the individual names of the deceased'. Inscription: the name of the dead person was, according to the formula of the sacramentaries, 'written before the altar'. Recitation: it was written down only so that, periodically, it could be solemnly spoken aloud. However, if the monks were made responsible for serving the dead and for disarming their wrath, it was above all because, closer than all mortals to the choir of angels, they were best placed to assist souls to rise towards the light, escaping the grasp of the 'black serpent' referred to in the epitaph of Dhuoda. It was still necessary for their prayers to please the Almighty, hence for them to appear in his eyes without stain. The princes who entrusted them with their own body and with the souls 'of their ancestors took pains, accordingly, to see that they were indeed pure. I see this as one of the reasons, and perhaps the most pressing, for the reform of the ecclesiastical institution which was gathering pace with the approach of the year 1000. During the eleventh century, at any rate, lords great and small spent lavishly to purchase the assistance of monastic prayers for the deceased of their blood. They gave generously to the old abbeys and they built many new ones. As an example of the function performed by these private monasteries, let us look at that of Andres, which was founded by Count Baldwin I of Guînes.

In 1079, out of piety, or to redeem a grave fault by the trials of the long pilgrimage, this warrior left for Compostella in the company of one of his friends. On the way, they stopped at Charroux. Dazzled by the magnificence of the services celebrated in this abbey, the two pilgrims each conceived the idea of founding an abbey of their own, back home. In return for a generous donation, the rulers of the great Aquitaine monastery promised Baldwin they would send him an abbot and a team of monks as soon as he had made the necessary preparations to receive them. In 1084, the little band of Benedictines settled at Andres, within a stone's throw of the castle of Guînes. By this foundation, Baldwin hoped to earn himself divine favours on a permanent basis. At the same time, he was asserting the independence of his house with regard to the nearby abbey of Saint-Bertin, and, in so doing, with regard to the counts of Flanders, who retired there to die. Lastly, the master of the land of Guînes consolidated the structures of the dynasty. He created a family necropolis; a privilege of Pope Paschal II specified that 'in this place, the sepulchre will be totally exempt in such a way that, according to their wishes, there will be buried there all the descendants of the count and all the peers of the castle'. Manassé, Baldwin's son and heir, was duly buried close to his father. When he had fallen ill, the monks had received him in their infirmary. Wearing a monastic habit, he had died in their midst; he was buried in the church in the presence of his wife and his vassals. All Manassé's brothers, with the exception of one who became count of Beirut and died in the Holy Land, joined him, along with several of his companions in arms. Gathered around the comital tomb, more than a dozen dead knights formed an immobile and silent court, an exact counterpart of the roving and boisterous court that had assembled around the living count.

Manassé left no son. He had done everything in his power to thwart the designs of his nephew, Arnold of Ghent, who aspired to succeed him. When close to death, the resentful Arnold had no wish to repose at Andres, alongside his uncle. He made generous bequests to Saint-Leonard, a nunnery where Manassé's widow was buried; she, in fact, had assisted his accession to power. Perhaps influenced by the new forms of piety popular in the second half of the twelfth century,

Arnold chose to be buried in a charitable institution, the hospital of Saint-Inglevert. It was there, sensing the end was near, that he relinquished his military equipment, his horse, his dogs and his falcons, 'everything that had given him pleasure in the world'. Not long after, however, death caught him unawares in a distant land, near Folkestone. Arrangements were hastily made to transport his body across the Channel. But the winds were adverse and the body arrived partly decomposed. The monks of Andres were delighted. Count Arnold had been punished. He should have come to them, as was right and proper. He had acted 'both contrary to what his ancestors had instituted and contrary to the rights of the abbey'.

His son, Baldwin II, respected those rights. On 2 January 1206, nearing seventy years of age, 'having disposed of his property, devoutly fortified with the rites of the Church, trusting in the mercy of the Lord', he had breathed his last in his house at Guînes. His eldest son was absent. His daughter-in-law, 'with excessive speed . . . eager to become countess', instructed the abbot of Andres to receive 'his lord and patron' as soon as possible and to prepare 'to welcome all those members of the family who would come to the funeral'. The monks thought this haste was indecent. They complied, nevertheless, out of fear of the husband. The body of the 'father of the country' was therefore carried to the place where, 'at a later date, the said lady [performing her role as woman, caring for the dead] had a double cross of stone erected for the count and for his wife'. After a short pause, the body of Baldwin was taken into the abbey church. The doors were left open and 'from evening until well into the night, a banquet was served to the knights and their ladies, to the townspeople and to others. Until the hour of the burial, they were provided with food and drink', gathered round the catafalque, feasting in the company of the still present dead man, and, as long as the corpse of the count remained exposed before the high altar, 'an innumerable multitude of poor was fed bread and meat brought from the various comital estates'. The heir at last arrived. He soon favoured the monastery with a tax exemption. In return, every year, until the end of time, the monks would celebrate a funeral service for the soul of his father.

We should note that reference to the spiritual is almost entirely absent in this account. The author of the chronicle, a Benedictine monk, mentions only a body around which the community, *dealbata*, in white, intoned the *planctus*, the customary lament. He mentions a meal, eating and drinking, and heartily, one last time, alongside the deceased; the feast appears to constitute the main element in the ritual. We have, therefore, a procession and a banquet, as at a wedding, and as in the ceremonies celebrating the entry of a son into knighthood. Entering the ranks of the dead happened in a similar fashion, with great pomp and amidst a similar profusion of victuals. Lastly, there was the tomb, the open grave and, above all, what mattered most, the obligatory placing of the corpse in the series of ancestral tombs.

To the masters of the land of Guînes, it seemed self-evident that the long cohort of the dead should be entrusted to the care of someone of their blood. They had been obliged to look outside the lineage for the first abbot, but the next would be one of them. They nominated Gregory, one of the great-nephews of Count Manassé, whose name destined him for the monastic condition. He was placed as a child in the family abbey, then, to prepare him to direct the community, he was sent to be educated at Charroux. 'Wishing to please the great men of the region, his relations', the monks of Andres elected him on his return. But the monks of Charroux, who knew him, insisted on another candidate. Gregory had to wait. Fourteen years later, he got the job. The chronicle of Andres describes him as 'of noble race, but not very enlightened, robust in body, benevolent to all, bound up in the ties of his earthly family and of military glory'. He spent much of his time goldsmithing. Four years later, he was deposed on account of 'his stupidity, his inertia and his inanity'. He was accused of being far too fond of skating in winter on the frozen marshes, like a layman, taking his monks with him. And then he had been caught 'plunging his hand in a lascivious manner down a woman's bodice'. By this time, the reform of the Church had made great progress.

There was no hesitation about ousting a black sheep. The family let it happen. What it cared about most was that its dead, sleeping below the tiled floor of the abbey, should be properly attended to.

In the religious houses where they prayed for the ancestors, and where their descendants gathered to honour them before coming to lie alongside them, the memory of the forebears became firmly fixed. It was there that it began to be put into writing and that the first authors of a literature that was entirely devoted to celebrating the glory of dynasties found not only material for their stories but compositional models. The lives of saints preserved near reliquaries, the 'legends' and the texts 'to be read' showed how to write the biography of a hero. The lists of popes, of bishops and of kings, the genealogy of Jesus in the Gospels and even the diagrams of affiliation produced in the episcopal courts during trials for incest showed how to connect one to the other the links in a lineage. Sometimes, the sequence of protectors of the monastic community was portrayed in the form of a tree. In a register of the abbey of Weingarten, for example, where they served the memory of the ancestors of the great family of Guelf, there appears a stem bearing, grafted on from generation to generation from the roots of the lineage, successive representations of a couple – and I mean couple: the face of a man appears next to the face of a woman and wife, a father and a mother are remembered together.

In the last third of the twelfth century, while artists were working on the enamel plaque destined to represent on his tomb, alive and brandishing his sword, Geoffrey Plantagenet, count of Anjou, the biography of this prince was being written by John, a monk of Marmoutier; what he was producing, in fact, to be read aloud periodically, was a 'legend' which differed little from a life of a saint. I suspect that few dead lords, however resounding their fame, enjoyed a rhetorical tribute as lavish as this one. Epitaphs, however, were common. The monks who were most gifted in literary composition, such as Raoul Glaber at Saint-Germain of Auxerre, the monk Martin at Saint-Jean of Montierneuf or the canon Gislebert at Saint-Waudru of Mons, were expected to compose them, and to restore them when the words engraved on the stone became illegible. These funerary inscriptions preserved the memory of a name, and this was their chief function. It is what Dhuoda had asked: that the passer-by might, before the tomb, spell out the letters of a name and speak it aloud in a short prayer. But Dhuoda had wanted more. She had embedded her name in the words of a poem. It became quite common, in fact, for the aide-mémoire to be expanded on the sides of the sepulchre. In the middle of the twelfth century, a clerk in the service of Henry Plantagenet, Wace, who was then transposing the work of Dudo of Saint-Quentin into the Romance language, described in his own way the funeral of Rollo. He mentions the tomb of this prince, about which Dudo had said nothing, but which Wace had seen in the cathedral of Rouen, in one of the side aisles of the choir, at the south end:

> The sepulchre is there and the epitaph, too,
> Which relates his deeds and how he lived.

It told a story, then, the rudiments of a history.

Wace was writing not in a religious house but at a court. The genealogical literature from which I am attempting to draw out a few portraits of women germinated in cloisters, among books pored over by monks and canons, and in monastic crypts, before rows of tombs, but it was in courtly society that it blossomed. Should we see this shift as a reversion to the profane of the ritual declamations to the memory of the ancestors, in an inverse movement from that which, three centuries earlier, had taken them into the abbey churches? Such a reversal might be encouraged by the retreat of monasticism, the greater intimacy of religious practices and the consolidation of family structures. But we know too little about lay funerary customs and, more generally, about what happened in the privacy of households to conclude that the dead on whose behalf the monks had been conscripted to chant were consequently no longer evoked within the family circle. I am myself persuaded of the opposite, and I feel sure that every head of household still dutifully recited the family saga to his children, his nephews and the sons of his vassals. Or else he devolved this responsibility to specific men of his blood, appointed guardians of the memory, such as the brother of Richard I of Normandy who was Dudo's informant, or that boy who, on rainy days, recited before his cousin Arnold, lord of Ardres, and the new knights who were his friends all he remembered of the exploits of his ancestors. There was a shift, certainly, but it was of a different order. If the lineage, or household, itself became, in the twelfth century, in the phrase of Howard Bloch, a 'producer of signs', signs which are not altogether obliterated today, and if it was in the courts that solid literary constructions, a few fragments of which still survive, were built, to confer renown on a family, it was the consequence of a shift that was cultural.

In the middle of the twelfth century, knightly culture emerged from the shadows, asserting itself against priestly culture. Priests were no longer the only ones with access to fine writing. The high nobility was now literate, or rather was once again literate, since this is what Dhuoda had been. Men capable of composing poems and of transcribing them onto parchment were now pensioners in the great houses. It was they who were the agents of the apparent shift from the monastery or chapter to the noble house, in fact a shift from the oral to the written word. What people sang in the courts, the 'songs of the *jongleurs*' which canon Lambert of Wattrelos said, in 1170, had kept alive the renown of those valiant knights, the brothers of his maternal grandfather, and the *chansons de geste*, which teemed with proper names (they were those of the mythical paladins, but since most of them belonged to the great families, many people hearing them spoken liked to think they referred to the most glorious of their ancestors), this collection of epics, whose sequences were transmitted from mouth to mouth, constituted a memory bank; it was rich in a different way from that of which the monks were guardians, and it was much more vivid in the minds of the men of war than the writings crammed into book-cupboards at the entrances to cloisters.

It was a rich treasure, in the care of professional singers. They added to it, inserting new names in order to please their patrons. They were as powerful as the public relations industry or the gossip columnists of today. William the Marshal was well aware of how, by publishing his virtues, the *jongleurs* enhanced his fame, and he showered favours on them. Whereas, in the house of Ardres, they complained bitterly about those singers who remembered that the head of this family had once refused one of them some much-coveted scarlet hose, and treacherously omitted, when they sang crusading songs, the name of the ancestor who had fought so bravely under the walls of Antioch. This treasure, nevertheless, was fragile, and much less resistant to the passage of time than the epitaphs or the saints' lives. The majority of these ephemeral words were lost just at the time when people were beginning to write them down.

At this period, the mid-twelfth century, in the course of an evolution which resulted in the restoration of the state, the primacy of the king of France was beginning to be asserted. The independence of the princely dynasties was challenged, and they defended themselves, falling back on that break-water, that primordial foundation, the memory of ancestral glory, guarantee of legitimacy and of the free possession of a patrimony. To make offerings to the monks so that they would do their best to keep the *memoria* alive was an act of piety. To consolidate the structures of a genealogy became a political act. To recall the exploits of the ancestors, and the rights they had conquered and held at the point of a sword, was to stand up more firmly to the pretensions of a rival power. Literary monuments were therefore built like ramparts.

And monuments they were; they had to be imposing, magnificent and covered with decorative detail, as had been the triumphal arches of the Romans, and as now, increasingly often, were their own tombs. To this end, they turned to established writers, to 'masters' who had been trained in the schools in the arts of discourse, in grammar and rhetoric – that is, to men of the Church. But the heads of families gave their commissions not to monks, who were trapped in their own liturgies, but to clerks. They were able to attract into their houses these men of written culture, who, once incorporated into the household, would be compliant. Their writings were, in the full sense of the term, domestic, made and used at home. Life in the rich houses was not without its attractions. In order to win the favours of the patron, to sit at his table, close enough to seize choice morsels, these skilled craftsmen employed all their expertise. As was expected of them, they expressed what the master thought, and what he wanted to be remembered, in a ceremonial language, that of the lives of saints, of the epitaphs and of the prayers that were sung amidst the fumes of incense around the catafalques. They wrote in Latin, the precious Latin of the twelfth-century renaissance, bombastic, cluttered with hyperbole. Then, with the passage of time, some of them, in the more open courts, began to employ the language of the young literature of entertainment, the Romance dialect, the sophisticated idiom by which the well-born liked to distinguish themselves from the common people.

These writers were capable of gathering their information from the writings of the past. We can see that they had dug into the coffers packed full of charters and searched in the cartularies and chronicles for material with which to flesh out and prolong the living memory. But for them, as for those who employed them, this scholarly labour remained subsidiary. What was required of them above all was that they put into a solemn and durable form the half accurate, often vague and sometimes extravagant memory that the men of the family held in their heads, they alone being qualified, by virtue of the blood which flowed in their veins, of evoking and of convoking, of making the dead of their lineage more present by repeated words. The hired writers collected these words and ennobled them by transposing them into the Latin of the liturgies. Modelling themselves on the royal genealogies, they arranged the story around an axis, the family tree, beginning with the founder, rising from generation to generation up to that of the patron. Modelling themselves on the lives of saints, they arranged along this axis vignettes similar to those which decorate the Weingarten manuscript, pictures of men and pictures of women, in fact biographies.

With regard to these texts, a number of questions arise: when, how, where, in what circumstances, by what medium, and before what audience was their content communicated? We have no answers. We know nothing of the modalities of the 'performance', or of the way in which, inside the house, the memory stored and idealized in this way was employed. We may at least suspect that there was a widespread desire among noble families to accumulate this memory for the use of those who would come after, the descendants, for their moral edification, so that they would not 'degenerate', so that they would remain as noble as their forebears. We may suspect that they wished also to reaffirm their rights, to confirm them in their power. I believe that there was a great flowering of this literary genre, and not only around the masters of the strongest principalities. But only snatches of it survive. This is hardly surprising. Most of the dynasties celebrated by these poems died out. The books composed to their glory lost their interest. They were neglected and almost all of them have perished. A few fragments have nevertheless lingered on, usually in a single late manuscript, a copy commissioned by the distant heirs of very old lordships, towards the end of the Middle Ages. These relics are rare but very valuable, the most faithful witnesses to what the noble houses of the twelfth century thought about themselves. We see in them, in particular, the reflection, though fleeting and indistinct, of the image that I am attempting to reconstruct, the image of women in the minds of the knights of the twelfth century.

4

Remembering Women

I t might seem paradoxical to turn to the literature of family in the hope of finding information about women. Lineage, after all, was a man's business. It was the business of those men who, by the emission of their semen, procreated the son destined to succeed them as head of the family when they had quitted this world and who, to this end, had married the woman procured for them by their father, and had impregnated her. This was their duty, as the wedding ritual made plain. Baldwin II, Count of Guînes, arranged the marriage of his eldest son. At the end of the day, while the celebrations continued outside in the gathering dusk, and while the host of guests were still making pigs of themselves, boozing and guffawing at the obscene pranks of the entertainers, the count went to the house of the new couple and entered the bedroom. The marriage bed had been decorated, adorned almost like an altar; the priests had duly incensed it and sprinkled it with holy water as, a few years later, on the death of the count, they would incense and bless in the church the litter on which his corpse was laid. The spouses were already there, in bed, prepared for their amorous duties. Raising his eyes and his arms to heaven, Baldwin called down on them the favours of the Almighty. What did he ask? 'That the seed should multiply all the length of the days and the centuries.' *Semen*; this Latin word, I am aware, means lineage, descendants. But it denotes first that concrete thing, that humour, the sperm. The fear of all heads of families, the nagging anxiety which gnawed away at Manassé, great-uncle of Count Baldwin, and turned his hair prematurely grey, was 'that no seed from their own body would survive'. These lords thought, obviously, in terms of sons. Manassé, who was obliged to 'beg an heir from one of his sisters', regarded the boy as 'of a foreign seed', since his mother had been made pregnant by a man from another lineage. When a lord referred to his ancestry, consequently, what came first to mind was the image of his forefathers, of those men who had effectively sowed the seed of their successors in the womb of their wife. He pictured knightly figures, roaring in the tumult of battle, infatuated with their exuberant virility.

A similar fixation on masculine values is strikingly apparent in the account that Fulk Réchin set out to dictate in 1096, reciting his own genealogy in order to prove that he held the county of Anjou legitimately. 'I, Fulk, Angevin count, son of Geoffrey of Château-Landon and of Ermengarde, daughter of Fulk, Angevin count, and nephew of Geoffrey Martel who was the son of that same grandfather of mine Fulk and the brother of my mother [right at the beginning, the count locates himself in relation to the two men from whom he had inherited the "honour", the power of command which had been challenged], I have decided to commit to writing how my ancestors acquired and held their honour up to my time, and then how I have myself held this same honour, assisted by divine mercy.' The aim is clear, and it is political: to attest to rights, the great lord speaking himself, and it is possible that the very simple, bare Latin of the text comes directly from him, and that, like many princes at the end of the eleventh century, he was literate enough to dispense with the intermediary of an ecclesiastical translator. This testimony is exceptional. It reveals how a man of war saw his genealogy at this period. Fulk expounds the memory, he says, as 'it was told to me by my uncle Geoffrey Martel'. This memory may have been to some extent refreshed by the clerics in the count's service, who had searched through old

charters in their quest for material to support his prerogat-
ives. We should note, nevertheless, the way in which
memory was normally transmitted. It was the head of the
house who kept it alive among the young men he maintained
in his household, and in particular in the mind of the one he
knew would, after him, be responsible for the honour, that
is for the patrimony as a whole, the lands, the power and the
capital of glory accumulated over the centuries. It was his
duty to relate the exploits of his ancestors before they were
forgotten, and to praise their courage, their physical strength
and their loyalty, all the knightly virtues of which they had
given proof.

The memory here goes back a very long way, for seven
generations. It extends exactly to the limits of that inordinate
sphere within which the ecclesiastical authorities prohibited
incest, forbidding the descendants of a same ancestor from
marrying each other. Such a requirement made it necessary
for the great families, those on which the bishops kept a
close eye, to remember at least the names of their very remote
forebears. Whenever a daughter was given in marriage, it
was prudent, in order to avoid indictment in a Church court,
to be in a position to present the prelates with a genealogy
which was also constructed on seven stories. In the monastery of Saint-Aubin of Angers, five documents of this type –
five lists of ancestors – were preserved. I assume that they
were drawn up on the occasion of the numerous remarriages
of this same Fulk Réchin, a man who kept changing his wife.
All of them place at the seventh degree, at the source of the
'seed', a certain Enjeuger. We know from other written
sources that this man lived some 150 years earlier. In his
account, Fulk also calls him *primus*. He follows his name
with three others, those borne by his son, his grandson and
the latter's son. No more is said about these very remote
forefathers. 'I am unable', Fulk confesses, 'to commemorate
worthily the virtues and the deeds of these counts because
they are so distant that the places where their bodies lie are
unknown.' In the absence of tombs and epitaphs, the memory
soon fades, remaining vivid for only a century. In the case of
the three counts who had preceded him, Fulk is able to recall

the 'deeds', the battles in which they had triumphed and what they had done to the benefit of the honour. In fact, the honour, the Angevin principality and its destiny, is what it is really all about. Men perished, but it survived, transmitted from hand to hand. These were male hands, obviously, strong enough to defend it and to push back its frontiers, the hands of valiant knights, brandishing the sword of justice and peace which had been solemnly handed to them when their adolescence came to an end. The whole of this history is a history of men. Fulk did not bother to name the wives; they had not held the honour. Remarkably, however, he says nothing further about his father either, beyond his name. This is because nothing remained to him of the powers that had been Geoffrey of Château-Landon's in Gâtinais; Fulk had sold them off, surrendering them to the king of France in order to secure investiture in a much more substantial inheritance, the county of Anjou. The only ancestors who deserved, in his eyes, to be remembered were those of his mother, the only woman who is named in this long account. Her name appears twice at the beginning of the document. In fact, everything Fulk held had come to him from her. She had given him the blood of the Angevins, and it was thanks to this blood that he exercised his power legitimately.

This was the essence and what makes the histories of families so precious for anyone who seeks to understand the position of women in the twelfth century. The woman's belly was not simply a receptacle. The seed deposited there by the man did not ripen on its own. This tender shell secreted its own humours. Within it, the blood of a woman mingled with the blood of a man, and her own semen joined his, since, as is clear from many indications, it was then generally believed that a female sperm existed. *Semen eorum*, 'semen of the two spouses', wrote the author of this genealogical account, a man who weighed his words and who had read treatises on natural history, when he came to reconstruct the prayer of Baldwin of Guînes before the marriage bed of his heir. Because the role of the wife was so decisive in the gestation, the son might aspire to seize the rights held by this mother's father. If the latter had no male descendant, he inherited her property, and sometimes, as in the case of Richard Coeur de Lion, son of Eleanor and grandson of William of Aquitaine, this property was immense. At all events, he inherited from her the virtues and the renown, which was what made maternal blood valuable. This woman who had carried him in her womb had been the bridge between two lineages, between the house she had left and the house to which she had been conducted with great ceremony on the day of her marriage, in the hope that she would soon be pregnant. She was the link, the *copula*. True, as a tool of the alliance, the woman was an object, but an object, given what it carried, of exceptional value: that of those daughters and sisters and nieces that the good lord distributed as rewards among the young warriors he educated and from whom he expected to receive faithful service, and that of the women of his seed that it was his duty to implant through marriage in other houses. In this way, he attached them to his own house, since, in the next generation, the sons resulting from these unions would venerate the same ancestors as he did. If the genealogical memory fanned out and often went further back on the maternal than on the paternal side, and if women necessarily occupy a place in this memory, it is not because it was women who were primarily responsible for it; the majority of the names listed by Dhuoda were those of men. The female forebears were present by reason of the role they had played in the destiny of the lineage. When the jurors came to recite a genealogy before the bishop in order to confirm or to demolish a presumption of incest, they had to name them too, and the literature of family could not omit the names of at least some women.

There were two reasons why their memory remained strong in this literature. The first was the strength of the affective link which, in this society, bound the son to his mother. As a general rule, a boy was sent away at a tender age from the house of his birth, as Dhuoda's son had been. His father soon became a stranger to him, and later a rival when, growing up, he longed to make free with the profits of lordship. In contrast, he clung to the memory of the mother from whom he had been wrenched and for whom he remained imperishably nostalgic. He venerated everything connected with this woman, including her dead ancestors. The second reason is stronger: among the majority of couples, the man was of less high extraction and less wealthy than his wife. Such a disparity between a couple seemed natural. When it happened that a father gave his eldest son a wife who was not above but below him, he felt the need to justify himself. This had been the case when Baldwin of Guînes had married the daughter of the lord of Ardres, his father's vassal. Describing this event some fifty years later, the house historian did not mince words. He spoke with regard to this marriage of 'humiliation'. The excuse was the perpetual peace that must at all costs be established between two houses which had confronted each other for centuries, much to the detriment of the surrounding countryside; in analogous circumstances, 'many nobles, dukes and even kings and emperors had agreed to demean themselves in this way'.

That the wife was usually more noble than her husband was a consequence of the state of the marriage market. It was unbalanced: a plethora of daughters on offer, a shortage of sons to take them. Heads of families did everything they could to marry off all the women in their power. Often, however, some remained on their hands. Henry, castellan of Bourbourg, who had five daughters, managed to marry only two of them, the other three remaining virgins till their death in the little nunnery attached to his castle. It had been founded for this purpose, to accommodate surplus women. According to Gislebert of Mons who, in 1196, wrote their genealogy, the counts of Hainault had better luck. With two exceptions, all the young women and wives in their family were, during the course of the twelfth century, married and remarried. Baldwin IV gave his sisters, his nieces and his female cousins to the knights who held the castles of Mons and Valenciennes in common, thereby assuring the loyalty of all who counted in the locality. 'In his lifetime, in full possession of his powers, he married his three daughters to three valiant warriors, though for a long time', added Gislebert, 'no one had heard of a count of Hainault who had either seen one of his sons a knight, or married one of his daughters.' It was one of the main aims of the father of the family to insert all his progeny into the social fabric: the girls by marriage – or, to be more precise, by legitimate maternity, since a woman at this period had no utility or real social existence as long as she was not a mother – and the boys by dubbing, the handing over of arms.

In the case of boys, however, it was not by marriage, since heads of families, afraid of seeing the ancestral patrimony fragmented and divided after their death between the sons of their sons, were reluctant to allow more than one of them to set up house. This prudence was effective; my documents reveal very few genealogical trees which had not grown in a straight line, without adventitious branches, until around 1180; it was at this period that restrictions on the marriages of sons began to be relaxed, since the circulation of money, flowing increasingly freely, liberated noble fortunes from some of their rigidity and made it easier to buy an establishment for a younger son. Until then, however, it was those with boys who had the advantage, selecting from among so many daughters on offer. They chose the best option, either the best blood or the largest dowry, preferring, obviously, eldest daughters without brothers or uncles, who might reasonably be expected to inherit. Occasionally, women who were sold to inferiors in this way by their father or brother objected. John of Marmoutier, embellishing the history of the counts of Anjou, and backdating by two centuries attitudes and events he saw around him, imagines the disappointments of an orphan, the daughter of a count of Gâtinais. When the latter died, the king of France, his lord, offered the little girl, along with the inheritance, to the chamberlain of the comital house, a man he could trust. She refused, protesting. It was indecent, she cried, to 'impose on her' a husband of such low status. The king handed her over to his wife, and the queen soon persuaded her to see reason. Usually, however, daughters passed from one house to another without breathing a word. It had been drummed into them that they should be obedient and most of them were betrothed very young. The two families usually made the agreement long before they were of marriageable age; the daughter of the count of Namur was barely a year old when Henry of Champagne, after the betrothal ceremony, took her back to his own house, only, in fact, to forget her as soon as a more advantageous match presented itself.

The case of these child-brides reveals with brutal clarity what purpose marriage served, why daughters became wives and what they were for men: bodies to be given and taken, put in reserve on account of the quality of their blood, thrown on the scrap heap when they were of no further use. At all events, as a result of these practices, eldest sons, the future heirs, mostly married above them, and when one of their younger brothers managed to marry, he, too, took a wife of higher rank than his own. This was because she was received as a reward from the patron he had served, who, to make himself better loved, granted him a maiden from his own family, hence of greater nobility. In short, the negotiations between families and the strategy of the great lords generally resulted in placing the woman in a position of superiority within the conjugal couple, and consequently, because of the prestige she had contributed, in assuring her, after her death, of the veneration of her descendants.

In the history of the lords of Amboise, we find the name of one woman, Denise. The anonymous canon who compiled this text around 1155 accompanied this name with a ringing eulogy, for which there were three reasons. First, this woman was very rich, thanks to her uncle, Geoffrey of Chaumont – he was a curious character: on account of the astonishing beauty of his body, he was surnamed the Maid; in fact, he never married, but became a knight errant after leaving all his property to his niece; he followed William the Conqueror in 1066, becoming, as a result, extremely wealthy, and from then on, on all his comings and goings between Normandy and the Loire Valley, he lugged with him a great treasury of gold and silver, which he drew on, in 1096, to equip Denise's son who was leaving for Jerusalem. Second, Denise had proved herself amenable, as all girls should, accepting the husband who had been chosen for her. Yet he was much inferior to her; he was the son of a vassal of the count of Anjou, Geoffrey Martel, who, victorious in 1044, had seized

Denise, like a spoil of war, from her uncle, Geoffrey the Maid, in order generously to reward one of the principal architects of his victory. Lastly, once married, Denise had played her part perfectly and provided, as all wives should, the son who would inherit the property and the glory of his ancestors. The eulogy was there so that her memory would be piously preserved within the family.

When men of the Church, better able to bolster memory with the contribution of written sources, came to describe their own ancestry, we see even more clearly what so many men of the twelfth century owed to their female ancestors. Around 1170, at Saint-Aubert-de-Cambrai, Lambert of Wattrelos compiled some *Annals*. Reaching the year 1108, the year of his own birth, he decided to say 'from whom he came'. He gave an account of himself. At the age of seven, he had left the house where he had been born. His maternal uncle, the abbot of Mont-Saint-Eloi, had come to ask 'his mother to give him to him'. It was to his mother, not his father, that the request was made – that is, to the woman who had carried the child in her womb, who had suckled him and to whom the child belonged much more than to his father. It was she who made the decision, and it was to someone of her own lineage that she entrusted her son. We see here the power that maternity conferred on wives: they were powerful through their sons. But the story shows also what confirmed this power. Its strength derived from the fact that, in this family, all the wives had been of better birth than their husband. Lambert remembered this. The estate where he had been born was the inheritance of his paternal grandmother; his grandfather, a younger son without fortune, had settled there. And the lineage of his mother was clearly superior to that of his father. Honour, everything of which Lambert was proud, the relations to whom he owed his career in the Church, all came to him from his mother, from his 'sweet mother', Gisla. She was the daughter, he said, of a 'very rich' man whose ten brothers had perished in the same battle, and a century later the *jongleurs* still celebrated their valour. Like so many others, this man probably owed at least part of his wealth to his wife. Born, according to Lambert, of 'the very high blood of the Flemish nobility', this woman, too, had many brothers. Eleven of them had spread their 'seed' all over the region; she had been unable, therefore, when she married, to bring land, but she had come with male and female slaves and, above all, with an abundant capital of renown. The nobility of which her grandson was so proud derived essentially from this grandmother. On this side, the maternal side, in fact, his relatives included abbots, abbesses and a bevy of spirited warriors: Richard of Funes, who was standard-bearer of Count William Clito and lost his life at the battle of Axpoel, the 'very famous knights of Lampernesse', and an uncle who had died fighting for King Henry I of England.

It was also through women that Robert, abbot of the Cistercian monastery of Foigny, claimed to descend from Robert the Strong, ancestor of the Capetians: through his mother Adelaide, through his mother's mother Adela, through Adela mother of his grandmother, and through her mother Beatrice, daughter of Edwige, herself daughter of Hugh Capet. His cousin, Guy of Basoche, was also very clear as to the source of the bluest of his blood. He had received it through a series of women. In 1190, he told his sister's son that he was *ex materna* of imperial and royal stock: royal, because Hugh Capet was his ancestor through the same Edwige and the same Beatrice, great-grandmother of his mother; imperial, because the blood of the Ottonians had come to him through a granddaughter of Henry the Fowler; she was ancestor to the seventh degree of Adela, mother of his mother, who descended to the tenth generation – also through women – from Judith, daughter of Charles the Bald. Women, those daughters and widows so freely distributed by heads of families, given to men of lesser nobility in the interests of the family and from munificence, spread everywhere the blood of kings. A part of this blood, of the blood of Charlemagne, runs in our veins, in yours, perhaps in mine, at all events in the veins of many of us, many more of us than we imagine. It was very often transmitted through bastardy, by casual encounters, but it was sometimes also transmitted in the marriage bed by wives.

The regular predominance of the woman within the lawful couple, and the respect with which, however proud of their virility, however timorous and, consequently, scornful in front of women, the warriors surrounded their female ancestors – those good women, those noble wives who, they were repeatedly told, had contributed so greatly to the glory of their house – means that the very masculine genealogical literature allows us to see something of a few twelfth-century women. Below, I present what I have been able to learn from this literature and in particular from two of its rare survivals; one concerns the very great house of the dukes of Normandy, the other a more modest lineage, that of the counts of Guînes.

Part II

Wives and Concubines

1

The Genealogy of a Eulogy

I return, almost inevitably, to Henry Plantagenet. The most brilliant court in Europe congregated around this prince; he encouraged the rise of chivalric culture because it was opposed not only to priestly culture but to that austere and deeply sacral culture for which the court of his Capetian rival was the focus; and, to enhance the brilliance of the periodic assemblies of warriors and ladies before whom, briefly interrupting his interminable campaigns, he showed himself in all his power and largess, he maintained in his household the most talented and original writers of his day. Many poems were written to please him. Two of them provide me with much of what I seek.

Through his father, Henry was descended from the Angevin counts. On his mother's side, as was frequently the case among the nobility, he could claim more glorious ancestors. His mother, a granddaughter of William the Conqueror, was heiress to the dukes of Normandy and the blood of Rollo coursed through her veins; it was on the basis of the rights that were hers, and by demanding the inheritance of his grandfather, King Henry I, whose name he bore, that Henry Plantagenet had claimed the crown of England, seizing it in 1155 and presenting himself from then on as successor to the legendary King Arthur. He wished to erect an impressive monument to the memory of his Norman ancestors – one that would be worthy of them. He wanted their history to be written in Romance, the language that was spoken around his table. Benoît de Sainte-Maure undertook this task.

In about 1165, Benoît had offered King Henry II the immense *Roman de Troie*, inserting, in passing, a discrete eulogy to his wife Eleanor. It is a story full of feats of arms, celebrating the exploits of Hector and Achilles in the guise of chivalrous knights. But, knowing the tastes of his audience, the poet had judged it wise to introduce a few women into this long sequence of military episodes. These included warriors, the Amazons and their queen Penthesileia, but also lovers. He showed Medea, inflamed with desire, preparing to join Jason at dead of night in the great hall, among the sleeping knights, but recoiling before the indecency of such an act, luring him into her chamber and there giving herself to him. He showed Helen as she received the avowal of Paris and the gift of his heart. He showed the fickle Briseis, forgetting the love she had promised to Troilus, yielding to the advances of Diomedes. 'The mourning of woman is short-lived, she weeps with one eye and laughs with the other . . . the best of them are frivolous . . . they never think they do anything wrong. Whoever trusts them betrays and deludes himself.' Though deeply misogynous, the work nevertheless aimed to please the wives and the young ladies, describing gowns, mantles, mirrors and trimmings in great detail, and making the paladins, emerged for a brief moment from their shells, fall prey to the agitations of love. This romance was popular. Benoît de Sainte-Maure now applied his recognized talent to gratifying his protector.

He was familiar, however, with neither Normandy nor the ducal household. He had probably been part of the very heterogeneous household of the king-duke for some time, but he came from Touraine, a region dominated by the paternal ancestors of Henry Plantagenet. He would have been better placed to speak of them. Unable to draw directly on the memory sources of the Norman lineage, Benoît expanded, indeed heavily embroidered, what he found in the work of others. He shamelessly exploited the recent work of Wace.

Now Wace, or Guace, was a Norman; he came from Jersey and he had close and very ancient links with the ducal family. It seems that one of his ancestors had held the office of chamberlain at the beginning of the eleventh century under Robert the Devil. He himself was perhaps already *clerc lisant*, or 'reading clerk', responsible within the household of King Henry I for everything to do with writing. In any case, in 1155, at the time when Henry II was establishing himself on the throne of England, he had dedicated to Eleanor a *Roman de Brut* (that is, a romance of Brutus, mythical founder of the Bretons). Inspired by Geoffrey of Monmouth and his legendary history of the kings of Britain, this story recounts the adventures of King Arthur. It extols the brilliance of his court, harbinger of that of Henry Plantagenet, attracting to it all the knights of Britain and Scotland, 'the Franks, the Normans and the Angevins, the Flemings, the Burgundians and the Lorrainers'. In the continuation of this poem, Wace had recently – or so, at least, it seems, for the chronology of these works is highly uncertain – composed a *Roman de Rou* (that is, a romance of Rollo), a history of the dukes of Normandy. He had questioned members of the family and collected memories which had been handed down from generation to generation within it, and he had taken the rest from books, being careful, as a conscientious historian, to warn his audience when he passed from oral to written sources.

Wace had based himself primarily on a work in Latin which William, a monk of the abbey of Jumièges, had in 1070–1 dedicated 'to the pious, victorious and orthodox William, king of the English by the grace of the Supreme King'. This *Deeds of the Norman Dukes (Gesta Normannorum Ducum)* consisted of seven books, one for each duke; book II was devoted to Rollo, and book VII to William. Written soon after the conquest of England, this work was designed to bolster the legitimacy of a contested power. It aimed to demonstrate – as, a little later, the 'Embroidery of Queen Matilda' known as the Bayeux Tapestry would demonstrate – the rights of the Conqueror to succeed Edward the Confessor in the royal dignity and, above all, to prove that William the Bastard was the rightful heir to Normandy.

This demonstration occupies a good half of book VII. The monastic text of William of Jumièges is austere and condensed, as bare and as solid as the pillars and vaults of the Abbaye-aux-Hommes in Caen which was being built at the same time. It was frequently copied, in numerous writing workshops, and it survives today in forty-five manuscripts. Some of the churchmen who revised it set out to complete it, very soon after, in the lifetime of Duke William or immediately after his death. Elisabeth van Houts has made a close study of this progressive enrichment, first at Saint-Ouen of Rouen and Saint-Etienne of Caen in 1096–1100, then in the monastery of Saint-Evroult, where, around 1113, Orderic Vitalis rewrote book VII, expanding it with many interpolations (this is probably the version used by Wace), and lastly at the abbey of Bec. The prior of this house, Robert of Torigny, future abbot of Mont-Saint-Michel, developed this work in many ways. With him, attention shifted away from the princely dynasty towards the country's nobility, with a view to attaching its many branches to the ducal stock. Robert was keenly interested in genealogy at a time – the beginning of the twelfth century – when the requirements of the ecclesiastical authorities with regard to incest were reviving in families the memory of their ancestors.

William of Jumièges had himself drawn copiously on a book entitled *The Manners and Deeds of the First Dukes of Normandy (De Moribus et Actis Primorum Normanniae Ducum)*, which its author, Dudo of Saint-Quentin, had completed between 1015 and 1026. The work that Henry Plantagenet commissioned in honour of the ancestors of whom he was most proud was essentially based on this history, the oldest and one of the richest ever written in France to the glory of a princely dynasty. Dudo was one of the canons of the collegiate church of Saint-Quentin-en-Vermandois. He had probably been educated at Laon in the cathedral school; his work is dedicated to bishop Adalbero, and he addressed the latter as if he was his master, asking him to correct his work and to confirm by his 'authority' the quality of the book. Dudo was blessed with exceptional skill in the art of writing. He displayed great virtuosity in manipulating the complex, baroque Latin which was then in vogue. But he liked also to cultivate *sapientia*, the sacred science; he called it 'mystical', thus letting it be known that he was familiar with Greek, and locating himself in the direct line of the Irish scholar, John Scotus, whose glory, at the apogee of the ninth-century renaissance, had radiated from Compiègne, from the chapel of the emperor Charles the Bald, and whose books were preserved at Laon. At the beginning of his reign, the king of the Franks, Hugh Capet, made use of Dudo, eminent representative of Carolingian high culture, which was assuming new vigour around the millennium in the old Frankish kingdom. He sent him on a mission to Richard, the leader of the pirates of the lower Seine. Richard valued Dudo highly, and held on to him. Now ranked among the prince's familiars, Dudo 'wished, by reason of his innumerable kindnesses, to render him the *officium* of his service'.

Richard had been educated close to King Louis IV d'Outremer, 'nurtured' in the house of the sovereign, as Dhuoda's son had been in the previous century, and as was still the practice, in the palace, in the case of the sons of the most powerful families in the kingdom. The young Viking had returned dazzled by the brilliance of Frankish culture. In the last years of his princedom, he devoted himself to the restoration of learning in the episcopal cloisters of Normandy, firstly in Rouen, round Robert, one of his sons, whom he had made archbishop. He needed someone who would help him, as Alcuin had helped Charlemagne in a similar enterprise, a master who could speak well and think well. He could imagine no one better qualified than Dudo to perform this function. Dudo belonged to the order of canons whose role, as he explained it himself in his book, consisted of giving guidance to the rulers of the 'lay order', of instructing them, in particular, in the arts of language. The book that Richard asked him to write in 994, and on which he laboured for more than twenty years, is in part educative. It is a manual of rhetoric. With exercises in versification scattered throughout, it offers models of fine writing, for example the two poems in the preamble dedicated to Archbishop Robert.

When, however, Richard asked him to describe the manners and great deeds of his predecessors since Rollo, 'who had restored law in the duchy', what he really had in mind was an account of how the chiefs of the Scandinavian bands had acceded to the most refined forms of civilization. This process of acculturation had been initiated and supported by the duke's ancestors. This ought to be remembered, their action glorified and their memory exalted. Dudo found himself in the same situation as Benoît de Sainte-Maure. He did not belong to the family and he was not a repository of this information. A stranger, he had to seek his material from those who by reason of their birth preserved the memory of the ancestors. He heard the basic facts from the mouth of Raoul, count of Ivry, Richard's brother, whom he presents as the author of the 'account' on which the work is based. William of Jumièges confirms this: 'I have made use of the history of Dudo', he says, 'who sought information from Count Raoul'. That this came directly from a man of the same blood guaranteed the veracity of the account. All the same, Dudo, like Benoît and Wace, drew additional information from several books. These were Frankish works, the *Annals* of Saint-Bertin and of Saint-Vaast and the *Histories* of Flodoard of Reims. But he also used a text composed within the ducal household: the *Lament* of William Longsword. The chief interest of this short text is that it shows how the dead were celebrated in the great princely families at the end of the tenth century. William, Richard's father, had just concluded a peace with the count of Flanders when the latter had him assassinated by hired thugs. Victim of an odious crime, William was venerated by his relations and his followers as a martyr, a sort of saint, and, as in the case of a saint, a 'legend' was composed in his honour. The *planctus*, the lament that was sung around his tomb, was preserved by being put into writing. It was the embryo of this genre of familial literature. Dudo was inspired by it to recount, in his turn, 'the life, the deeds and the triumph' of this unhappy hero, 'in order', he said, 'by this account, to help others, but especially the descendants, the people of William's lineage, to rise towards celestial joys'. The whole work was constructed on the basis of this biography.

It began by evoking an extremely savage Norman chief, Hastings. Whether this man ever existed or not, he was not an ancestor. His image, that of the ravager who plunged the country into chaos, was probably invented, and it is placed at the beginning of the history because it was necessary to present as devastated, levelled and bare, as in the first days of the world, the site of the construction which the first three dukes, Rollo, William and Richard, would patiently, one after the other, erect. The purpose of the work emerges clearly in the way in which Dudo made use of the lament, and in the way in which he reworked and improved on this text, with scant regard for historical accuracy, but anxious to show what his patron wanted him to show and what his work was designed to do: to glorify a success story, the political and cultural integration, in stages, of the barbarians from the north into Latin Christendom as it had been modelled by the Frankish kings.

Richard did not live to see the book completed. It was his son who received it from the hands of Dudo. It is a fine work, at least for whoever is not irredeemably resistant to the manners of writing of the age. Positivist historians have scorned and continue to scorn it, heaping sarcasms on Dudo the fantasist or Dudo the manipulator. I believe this work to be a document of the highest value. I, too, am a positivist, in my way. For me, the positive is not the reality of the 'small true facts'; I am well aware that I will never achieve this. The positive is this concrete object, this text which preserves an echo, or a reflection, of words and of deeds irrevocably lost. For me, what counts is the testimony, the image that a man of great intelligence presented of the past, his omissions and his silences, how he handled memory in order to adjust it to what he thought, to what he believed to be true and right, and to what those who heard him wanted to believe was right and true. Thus Dudo, when he speaks of the mother of William Longsword or of the mother of Richard, does not perhaps tell the strict truth. I know this, and yet I value every word he uses. They reveal how people liked to picture their female forebears in a princely court, which was gradually, in the year 1000 emerging from savagery.

The interest of this work is all the greater in that it was re-used and interpreted for nearly two centuries. This happened first among monks, in the austerity of the cloisters of Normandy, in Latin prose, then among domestic clerks, in the animation of a court, in Romance verses, for the instruction and pleasure of the knights. Thus the memory reaches us set down in successive strata, and we are extremely fortunate in being able to trace how, over a long period, the way in which men imagined the women who shared the bed of the first dukes of Normandy kept changing.

2

The Trouble with Women

W omen play only a small role in this history of warriors, of men of violence gradually tamed. Always in the background, they were playthings in the hands of these brutes. When, descending on Neustria, destroying everything before them, the bands of the 'ferocious' Hastings had put the soldiers to flight, they turned on the poor, the defenceless, the clergy and the women. According to Dudo, all the young girls were cruelly ravished and all the wives were carried off. The victorious leaders kept those of the vanquished chieftains for themselves; they were the most precious and the sweetest part of the booty. But they were obliged to compensate their companions in arms as, later, did Canute the Dane, who, after taking London and seizing the widow of King Ethelred, 'gave for her to the whole army the weight of her body in gold and silver'. Occasionally, women dared to resist male violence. William of Jumièges refers in passing to those *pugnatrices* of Coutances who, it was said, one day, with blows from their pitchers, had knocked out some fearsome aggressors, Englishmen come to pillage Normandy. The fantasy of the amazon adding prowess to her bodily charms haunted knightly dreams. Both Wace and Benoît, accordingly, inflate out of all proportion the exploits of these 'fiery and savage' women. But they judged it prudent to signal clearly what was unusual, even shocking and subversive, in such pugnacity. It broke with the natural order of things. These female warriors 'seemed like women depraved'. As proof of this licentiousness, they appeared with their 'hair undone', flowing loose, flaunted as, at that period, was the hair of prostitutes. The seductive mane of hair was, in fact, the emblem of female powers, of that disquieting force whose intensity men knew only too well and which they felt obliged to stifle. In the well-ordered life, young girls' hair might float freely in the wind, but married women were expected to ensure that theirs was never seen. They kept it hidden under a wimple, imprisoned as they were themselves imprisoned, subject to the power of a husband. The idea of seeing them let down their hair, take up a weapon and brandish it struck terror into male hearts.

Women have a much greater presence, in fact, in the mid-twelfth century in the tales of the storytellers whose job it was to keep the court of Henry Plantagenet amused. Like their predecessors, they imply that it was women's destiny to be taken, still objects of male desire. But they repeat that this desire ought now to be mastered: seduction replaced rape. Women joined in the game of love. This is how they appear in three little stories that Wace incorporated into the history he was putting into Romance. The writers whose work he used provided him with the bare outlines of a portrait of Richard I. Wace added a few embellishments, drawn from the oral tradition, transcribing what had been passed down by word of mouth within the household concerning this very ancient ancestor. He warned his audience: what I say comes from long ago:

> I have heard it from many people,
> who had themselves heard it,
> but often from nonchalance,
> from laziness, from ignorance,
> many fine deeds remain to be written down.

In the case of some of these deeds, the silence had been deliberate:

for the sin the duke committed
when he killed the knight
this was not put into writing
but the fathers told it to the sons

These anecdotes are introduced to illustrate the virtues of
the good prince, primarily his wisdom. A new Solomon,
Richard is shown giving wise judgement in a very humdrum
case. A monk of Saint-Ouen had passed a lady in a Rouen
street. The sight of her inflamed his blood.

He was wild with love for her,
he desired her,
he would die
if he did not enjoy her.

He accosted her, and successfully sweet-talked her. The
game, played according to the rules, started with words:

He said so much and promised her so much
that the lady eventually agreed
to go to an inn that night

To reach the rendezvous, the gallant had to cross some water
in the dark by a footbridge. It was narrow and it wobbled.
He fell off and was drowned. The angel and the devil debated
which of them was to carry off his soul. The angel wanted it
for himself: the sin had not been committed, no one could be
sure that the dead monk would not, at the last minute, have
turned back. Was it fair to condemn him to eternal hell-fire
'simply for a foolish thought and a lack of willpower'? The
Church was at that time engaged in perfecting the sacrament
of penance. The unresolved question was: where did the fault
lie? Who was really responsible? In the end, the duke was
appointed as arbiter. He happened to be close by, in his
room, applying himself to his duties while his subjects slept,
as conscientious sovereigns do. What was needed, he said,
was to resuscitate the defendant. Let him be put back on the
bridge. If his first step was back home, he should be saved.

The miracle took place, and the culprit escaped hell-fire. But, in the morning, still wet through, he must confess his faults as a good penitent. In the second fable, Richard appears in the role of knight errant. He had ventured alone, far from the court, into one of those perilous expanses – in this instance, a clearing deep in the forest of Lyons – where the paladins of the romances customarily experienced strange encounters. From a distance, he saw a knight and a young lady, both of extraordinary beauty, lying full length in the heather. 'He had never seen such beautiful people together.' They were another Tristan and another Iseult. He did not know them. At the duke's approach, the knight rose and – an enigmatic reaction: we are in the realm of the marvels of courtly tales – killed his companion. At once, Richard felled him with a blow from his sword. He acted, admittedly, to redress a wrong, to avenge an abused woman. But he went too far; he ought to have remained in control of himself. This was his fault, the 'sin' that no one had previously dared to write down. The final episode does not involve Richard but one of his huntsmen, a man of the people; the setting is the same – wild nature, a forest, the realm of prodigies.

The three stories are interrelated. All three show how men should behave towards women, teaching courtly morality in matters of love. The requirements of this morality differ according to which of the three orders the man belongs. The first story tells of a monk: such men should not approach women. The second involves a knight: he had the right to love, but he should do so discreetly, concealing his name and that of the lady, risking all so that she should not be *honnie*, dishonoured; he ought also to master his desire for a long time, which is why, lying next to his love, his sword was placed between them, a frontier which must not be crossed; as for the girl, she had neither removed her wimple nor let down her hair; it was forbidden to a knight, lastly, to use violence against women of the nobility, to raise a sword against them. This was the crime which Richard had punished, but too drastically. The last male character belongs to the third estate. On the edge of the wood, performing his lowly duties, this serf had started the game bird of his dreams when he had come upon a pretty young girl. He wooed her, but, like the peasant he was, roughly. He rushed things, and took his pleasure by force, as knights took theirs from shepherdesses. At this point the fairy, because this is what she was, took hold of him and tossed him miraculously high into the air. To his shame, he was left impaled on the top of a tree, mortified. For he whose station in life made him make love like the animals had aimed too high; he should have been content with a woman of his own rank, another serf.

The lesson of these three anecdotes extends also to the duties of women. Those of quality – and the vocabulary employed ('married lady', 'young lady', 'maiden') makes plain that it is they alone who are at issue – ought to yield only to knights, who, for their part, were obliged to treat them according to the ritual that had been developed in the courts, primarily in that of Henry Plantagenet. Adapting in his own way what he had gleaned from domestic memory – and it is precisely this way and these adaptations which reveal the mental attitudes of the twelfth century – Wace sketches in a few strokes the image of women that was the norm among the men of his day. By their nature, women were weak. They needed special protection. 'Women should have peace everywhere'; these are the very words of the prescripts concerning women set down at the time of Dudo in the first oaths of peace imposed on the men of war. When women left the house, they should be accompanied by a man, or else they might freely be seized; they were, in the meaning given to the word in the twelfth century, *aubaines*, godsends. As for the girl raped by the huntsman: 'What was she doing alone in this wood?' Was she a whore? or a fairy? She was fated, in any case, because alone, without a male guardian, women, married or unmarried, were not only in danger of being seized, but were left to their own devices, hence to base instincts, and they inevitably abandoned themselves to lust, inclined as they were to the game of love. Lying in wait at the edge of a wood, the fairy, to take her pleasure, watched out for a passing man. Women were easy targets, soon beguiled by sweet words, then giving themselves altogether ('nothing was forbidden him'), but by this very fact they were traps into which men, seduced by their charms, their finery and the irresistible appeal of their flowing locks, fell. For all men, whatever their estate, women were both tempting and dangerous, a source of pleasure and a cause of perdition. I note also that Duke Richard is shown performing one of his major functions. As was expected of the princes to whom God entrusted the power to judge and to punish, he suppressed the disorder that was provoked by the presence of women. In his own household, in which men of all three orders rubbed shoulders, and in that immense household constituted by the principality over which he ruled, his prime duty was to regulate sexuality. All the written works composed to the memory of the dukes of Normandy say this.

It was Dudo's task to show how, in the course of a century, the Normans had been civilized. What was civilization? First, Christianity, then respect for the precepts which assured the reproduction of society through the balance of its edicts. For men, this meant an ordered way of sharing women. This is why, in the early pages, when he is describing the dreadful primitive disorder that the Viking chiefs, once they had been baptized, deserved credit for gradually mastering, the canon of Saint-Quentin gave sexual chaos pride of place. 'These men', he said, referring to the Scandinavian pagans, 'burned with an excessive ardour, every one of them defiled many mistresses with his odious copulations.' As a result, 'they fathered by these repugnant and illicit couplings innumerable descendants'. So we have polygamy and its consequences – too many children – and, eventually, a superfluity of young men, in itself a cause of turbulence: the clear-sighted Dudo recognized one of the most pernicious structural vices afflicting the world of his day, the unrest spread by 'the young', by the bands of unmarried knights. Transposing, he imagined gangs of youths – the word he uses is *milites*: knights – at the end of the ninth century. He pictured them confronting each other in incessant battles, even attacking old men, 'the fathers and the uncles', the epitome of subversion. Scandinavian society dealt with this problem by ritually expelling its young.

According to the 'ancient rites', it ejected them, launching them and their devastation against neighbouring countries, just as the war leaders who were Dudo's contemporaries, every spring, led a motley crew of youths out into the 'marches', the wild expanses which then separated the various principalities, so that they could give vent to their military ardour in those war games which were later called tournaments. This historian, writing in the year 1000, correctly recognized this periodic ejection of trouble-makers as the underlying cause of the Norse incursions into Christian countries. The first victims of such eruptions of violence were, naturally, women. The pirates, inflamed with lust, flung themselves on them. That the excesses of masculine sexuality were one of the most notable characteristics of a lack of culture was repeated, at the time of William of Jumièges, by William of Poitiers, author of a biography of William the Conqueror. Adapting the words used by Sallust of the Moors of Jugurtha, he said of the Bretons of Brittany, those doughty warriors whose dangerous attacks posed a constant threat to the Normans: 'In this country, a single knight begets fifty because, transgressing divine law and the rules of modesty, he possesses a dozen or more women.'

The companions of William the Bastard may secretly have envied them. At any rate, half a century later, Wace and Benoît de Sainte-Maure went further. Whereas Dudo's description of the lustful ardour of the Norsemen had clearly been abbreviated by William of Jumièges, they expanded it. They thought of their audience, of all those violent men in search of women, and knew how to hold their attention by portraying their distant ancestors as:

> so lustful and boiling,
> so full of desire and so ardent
> that the women were abandoned
> to them all and in common

So now we have not a stallion ruling over a herd of fillies, but the abolition of all rules, an undisciplined romp. Women 'in common', and an execrable mingling of the sexes; in the twelfth century, everybody said that the fiends of hell, mercenary soldiers from the dregs of society, heretics and marginals indulged in similar abominations.

> Few had one of them so dear
> that they did not have others, whores.
> When they intermixed like this
> and the one was abandoned to the other
> shamelessly, with no tenable law,
> and without fitting customs
> the son did not know his father,
> or who was his sister or who his brother.

Here, we detect a double echo, that of the sermons denouncing the dire consequences of the adulterous liaisons which confused family relationships, and that of the chivalric romances whose hero, ignorant of his ancestors, illustrated the fantasies that the fear of incest and illegitimacy aroused in the minds of the nobility of the day.

Such was the disorder when Rollo appeared. He was himself one of the 'young', an adventurer and a ravisher of wives. Fired by a 'virile virtue' which was vented in violence, he had swooped down on England at the head of a band of youths. But God had chosen him, guiding him, inspiring him and leading him across the Channel to 'that province he gave him'. Rollo made good use of divine grace. To a country bled dry, he restored security and prosperity. For he had freed himself from paganism, hence from savagery. In 911, King Charles the Simple had agreed that a part of Neustria should be subject to Rollo's power, demanding in return that he become a Christian. The baptism was a new birth. Regenerated by the baptismal water, Rollo changed from an aggressor to a protector and a civilizer.

During the seven days which followed his baptism, Rollo devoted himself entirely to sacred matters. Restoring the structures of the Church, he rebuilt the three cathedrals of Rouen, Bayeux and Evreux, and the three monasteries at Mont-Saint-Michel, Saint-Ouen and Jumièges, and showered gifts on Saint-Denis, the abbey protected by his godfather, the duke of France. On the eighth day, putting aside the white robe of the neophyte, he turned to profane matters and it was then that he married; marriage and civilization went hand in hand. While the girl, the daughter of King Charles, who had been promised before the peace was concluded, was being conducted to his bed, the duke began to rebuild the walls of the cities, promising security to all the inhabitants of the country, marking out 'with a cord' the lots which he granted to his friends, 'lastly enacting stable laws and rights'. There was to be no more violence and, very specifically, no more sexual violence. Rollo set the example. He submitted to the rules of conjugality. Dudo is expressing what was thought by his patron Richard I, as well as by his masters, the bishops of Franconia, Adalbero of Laon and Gerard of Cambrai, who were then endeavouring to suppress the disorder provoked by the sudden collapse of royal power. Attributing to Rollo the creation of that Norman peace which was quoted as an example in his day, and which, a few years later, would be eulogized by the Burgundian monk, Raoul Glaber, Dudo closely linked the enterprise of political reconstruction and the imposition of conjugal discipline. To emerge from chaos, to end disorder and to bring the land back into cultivation implied that the use of women must be strictly controlled and that sexual activities must be contained within well-ordered households, firmly directed by men who were responsible for their wife. Dudo illustrated his thesis with a little story.

As a symbol of the restoration of security, the duke had forbidden people to take their ploughs home with them; they were to be left out in the fields. A ploughman went home for his dinner, leaving his plough behind. Like many wives, his was wicked; she went and removed the beam, the share and the coulter. The peasant complained to the duke, who compensated him and ordered an inquiry in the village. There was recourse to the ordeal of trial by fire in the name of Jesus Christ, but without success. The newly baptized Rollo was worried, and asked the bishop: 'If the God of the Christians sees all, why does he not expose the culprit?' When questioned, the peasant revealed that only his wife could have known where he had left the plough. She was seized and whipped with switches. She confessed. (This story reveals in passing that only the men had been subjected to the ordeal; like domestic animals, women had no public status; they were objects, pieces of furniture.) The duke then said to the peasant: 'Did you know that your wife was the thief? Then you deserve death, and for two reasons: you are the master of your wife (these are the words of St Paul), you ought to keep her under control, and prevent her from doing harm. If, within the conjugal couple, the man is not at the helm, everything goes awry. What is more, you ought to have denounced her and handed her over to the justice of the people, so you are her accomplice.' The woman and her husband were hanged. The sentence was harsh, so harsh that William of Jumièges, a few years later, toned it down. By his account, only the wife was punished: her eyes were put out.

3

Wives

S ocial peace, then, rested on marriage. But what sort of
marriage, given that many types existed? When, during
the minority of Richard, grandson of Rollo, Louis
d'Outremer occupied Normandy, the Franks thought that
the way in which couples were formed in this savage foreign
country was not correct, and that they might therefore help
themselves to the wives of the Scandinavians. They may no
longer have behaved like the companions of Hastings, and
they did not pounce on women to satisfy their lust, but they
expected their leader to give them women. The king was
harassed by the *tirones*, the young warriors in his entourage.
'We have served you for a long time', they said, 'without so
far ever having received anything from you that satisfied us,
apart from food and drink. We beg you to expel the Normans
or else to exterminate them. You will then grant us their
wives and you will give us what they hold': the wife and, at
the same time, the land. One of the supplicants had his eye
on the wife of Bernard the Dane; she was very beautiful and,
above all, Bernard was very rich.

It is noticeable that William of Jumièges, a monk, skips
over this episode, whereas Wace and Benoît dwell on it at
length. According to Wace, when the king had given in and
promised the 'wife of the Dane' to the man who was asking
for her, 'all the others wanted to have their own and closely

examined the ladies throughout the country'. Louis assured
them that they would all be provided for; there was no
shortage of women of quality. But the latter did not let
themselves be taken so easily, and 'the terror of the women'
provoked a successful revolt against the occupiers. Bernard
the Dane kept his wife. What is remarkable in her case is the
way in which Benoît de Sainte-Maure lingers over what it
was about her body that made her so desirable to men.
Inspired by a single word in Dudo, *perpulchra*, 'exceptionally
beautiful', he composed fifteen verses spelling out and celebrating the freshness of her complexion, the delicacy of her
mouth and her sparkling eyes. 'There was no one who, seeing
her, would not have wished to hold her naked and enjoy
her.'

Like Wace, Benoît knew what was in the dreams of the
'bachelors', the knights without wives who were his most
attentive audience. They yearned for two things: pleasure
and an establishment, a woman and land. His patron, Henry
Plantagenet, exploited this longing to strengthen his hold on
them. He took care always to keep at hand, strictly supervised, an impressive reserve of marriageable women, the
daughters, mostly, or the widows of his vassals. They were
coveted by the young men of his court. In order to get their
hands on one, they behaved meekly towards their patron.
The future wives constituted a valuable currency with which
to buy friendships and peace. By distributing them, the good
lord established some of the *juvenes* in households, detaching
them from the bands of turbulent knights, turning them into
sober and settled *seniores*. Thus, by marriage and by the wise
use of women, the potential for disorder was gradually
reduced in twelfth-century France.

For a long time, women had also been the guarantee of an
equilibrium between states. It was by the exchange of young
girls that *pacifica conversatio*, peaceful relations, were established between princes and between nations. If, in the time
of William Longsword, son and successor of Rollo, the
accession of Normandy to Christian culture and to the
Frankish political zone gathered pace, it was because his
mother, who had been baptized, was a Frank and he there-

fore had 'a Frankish connection', and because he gave his
sister to a Frank, the count of Poitiers, and himself took as
his wife the daughter of Hugh of Vermandois, another Frank.
Dudo shows such alliances being concluded in the middle of
forested frontier zones, where war leaders, temporarily rec-
onciled, and united by vows and embraces, went deer-
hunting in each other's company. Half a century later,
Normandy was joined to Brittany by a mixed marriage.
According to William of Jumièges, the Breton Count Geoffrey wanted the 'friendship and aid' of Richard II. He went
to the latter's court with a large mounted escort. Richard
entertained him for a while, displaying his wealth and the
'magnitude of his power'. 'Would the tie of love between
them not be stronger', asked Geoffrey, if he married Richard's sister, 'a maid, beautiful of body and full of grace by
the virtue of her morals'. The duke consulted the great men
of the duchy and 'gave her to him in the Christian manner'.
Then, a little later, through an embassy, he expressed the
wish to acquire Geoffrey's sister. The count conducted her as
far as the frontier between the two houses, to Mont-Saint-
Michel, where Richard 'received her with all due honour and
bound himself to her by legitimate tie'. She gave him three
daughters. He married one to the count of the Burgundians
and a second to the count of the Flemings, and after the early
death of his brother-in-law, took Brittany into his custody in
his capacity as maternal uncle of the two orphans.

The need to keep the peace was one of the reasons which
compelled leaders of principalities to take a wife. But the
strongest reason was that they had a duty to marry so that
their house would survive, something Dudo brought out in
the case of William Longsword. As I have said, William was
remembered as a martyr; he was the saint in the family. He
is also presented as having been, from infancy, a seeker after
spiritual perfection. 'Devoting the time of his youth to Jesus
Christ', he longed to become a monk. 'His intention was to
subject himself to the abstinences of chastity. He resisted the
pleasure of fathering descendants.' In so doing, he was failing
in his obligations as a prince. Dudo portrays him as being
reprimanded by Martin, abbot of Jumièges. William ought

to renounce his idea of 'converting', of changing his status, because it was important that he remain in the *ordo* in which God had placed him. The country needed a man of the sword who would defend it against the pagans and the wicked, it needed a layman who was permitted and encouraged to copulate, in order to bring an heir into the world. When he received this advice, William agreed to take a wife, yielding to the prayers of his people and the exhortations of the great men. The latter were pressing: 'Renounce your vow. It is necessary to you and to us that a magnificent duke is born of your seed, we have need of your seed.' Here, we see the law of lineage expressed. It was a hard law for certain rulers who had little liking for relations with women, not from a saintly vocation but because they had acquired a taste for boys during their long apprenticeship in military company. This was the case with Henry I and with his grandson Louis VI in the lineage of the kings of France, and with William Rufus and Richard Coeur de Lion in that of the kings of England. In the case of Simon of Valois, St Simon, this repugnance was again presented as a desire for chastity, and he held his ground. The others married, as dynastic morality demanded.

All three of the first dukes of Normandy accepted this and took a legitimate wife. When King Charles the Simple made his peace with Rollo, his daughter Gisla was handed over to a Frankish archbishop as 'security for the bond of the oath and the confederation'. I should add that scholars are by no means sure that Dudo did not invent, if not this woman, at least her name; searching through the texts, they have found only one Gisla, and it cannot be her since she was a baby at the time; they are forgetting that daughters were given at all ages. The archbishop said to the Viking leader: 'Take her . . . by this union, you will enjoy descendants and you will hold the province for ever.' What marriage signified for adventurers without connections could hardly be put more plainly: the establishment of a dynasty in a territory. The companions of Rollo, too, advised him to take Normandy and the girl, both of them beautiful and promising. William of Jumièges thought it prudent to assure his readers that the husband led the wife 'to the union in his bed in the Christian manner'. Dudo had said nothing about a wedding.

The sister of William Longsword was given to the count of the Poitevins; when she left Rouen for Poitiers, the procession which accompanied her – with its sumptuously harnessed horses drawing her litter, more horses following behind and the 'marriage goods' she brought as dowry, a troop of slaves of both sexes and caskets and chests filled with silks and jewels – proclaimed the opulence of her brother and ducal magnificence all along the route and right into the great hall in which she was received. When, a little later, William married in his turn, now taking not giving a wife, he was still shown in the dominant position. It was not he, according to Dudo, who made the first move: he was sought out. The very powerful Hugh of Vermandois had noticed him 'glittering throughout Christendom by the virtues of his soul and of his body and by his great deeds'. Hugh offered him his daughter. The duke went to get her and escorted her back, but this time the story emphasizes not the dowry and the value of the fiancée, but the masculine, the horde of horsemen galloping around this female body, miming her abduction. What I find interesting, however, is not the inclusion of these detailed descriptions, but the astonishing fact that this woman, from whom it was hoped that the leader of the Normans would derive descendants, is never once named. It is as if her person – notwithstanding her descent from Charlemagne – counted for nothing in the ancestral memory.

Naturally, Dudo named the wife of Richard I, who had commissioned the work. She was Emma, daughter of Hugh the Great, duke of the Franks. Dudo presents the giving of this woman as a very clearly political act. The initiative came from Hugh. He first approached Bernard of Senlis, the young man's maternal uncle, in this case the matchmaker, since Richard had lost his father. Was another alliance projected? Would the Norman leader, if a pact was made, agree to 'serve' him, that is, become his vassal, and take him as defender of his land? The aim of the duke of the Franks was clear; he wanted to detach the young prince from King Louis, who had brought him up, a second father, and bind him directly to himself. Once the 'oath had been taken', Hugh gave up his daughter. Dudo thought it was necessary at this point to specify that he did not sell her, that this really was a 'conjugal union', a marriage treaty in the Frankish manner.

Emma was very young and Richard did not carry her away immediately. He made a commitment. And it is the way in which Benoît de Sainte-Maure, half a century after Dudo, imagines the acts marking the agreement that reveals what was customary in the courts at the time of Henry Plantagenet. Richard, he says,

> had received her as his affianced
> and sealed the agreement with his bare hand.

(We may note in passing the crucial gesture: the handshake, as at a market.) He would take her 'when the time was right'. The future husband was then made 'a new knight' along with squires of the same age, dressed in ermine and brocade. Hugh girded them with the sword 'and did not forget the touch on the shoulder': as patron of chivalry, his hold on his son-in-law would be stronger. Let us return to the original account. Time passed. On his death-bed, in the speech of farewell he made, as was the custom, to his companions in arms, the duke of the Franks reminded them that he had given his daughter to Richard on their advice and by their oath 'although she was of a tender age'. Let them hand her over to him as soon as she was 'ready for a man'. The Normans, for their part, 'were thinking of posterity'. They were afraid that 'the glory of descendants might be lacking to the husband and that a succession by his seed might be wanting'. They urged Richard to consummate the marriage. 'You bound yourself to this girl by the oath to join yourself to her; the oath remains; she is nubile; it is therefore right that you should sleep with her by the matrimonial tie.' Richard eventually agreed and preparations for the wedding began. Dudo describes this festival, which he calls 'licentious' and 'bawdy'. In fact, the union was sealed twice over: first, spiritually, between souls, by the oath and the exchange of words; then, often much later, on the wedding night, by the 'joining of the sexes', which the crowd of guests celebrated with much ribaldry. For Wace, who makes his own interpolation here, mixing the sacred and the profane, the ceremony took place in the palace at Rouen, the Holy Spirit then authorizing Richard to enjoy his bride:

> to hold her in his arms
> to kiss her eyes and her mouth.

Everything had been done according to the rules. Hugh the Great 'could not have made better use of Emma'. His followers had taken care to see that the pact had lasted until 'the child was led to the man'.

Dudo conscientiously praises the three legitimate wives. In the case of Gisla, he first assures us that she was 'properly born of the seed of each of her progenitors', which, in this polygamous society, was a not unimportant quality. He portrays her as beautiful and tall, a virgin, of course, of good counsel, amiable, easy to get on with and, lastly, which is worthy of note, 'very skilful in the work of the hands'. The same is said of the nameless woman for whom William Longsword agreed to abandon his intended chastity; she, too, was 'expert in all the tasks which are incumbent on women'. The praise is more specific in the case of Emma: 'Well suited to the courtesy and the nobility of her husband', who 'abounded in virile power and fecundity', this maiden with generous curves was built 'to give him pleasure', 'perfectly made for conjugal embraces and for the caresses which make bed delightful'. This canon, writing in the year 1000, knew what his patron wanted him to do: to exalt in his own wife and in the wives of his forefathers the ability to give sexual pleasure, that skill in the acts that men expected of women and which made agreeable the task imposed on heads of families, the impregnation of the girl that the Holy Spirit had placed in their bed.

Not one of the three women who shared the bed of the dukes of the Normans, however, was, or became, a female forebear. In the case of Gisla, it may be that she never reached the 'proper age', or that Rollo never slept with her, and that she remained what she had always been, simply a 'guarantee'. Dudo, reporting what people said about her, suggests that the wife remained unsatisfied. He shows her in Rouen, complaining to emissaries from her father who had come without her husband's knowledge. The latter's friends warned him and urged him to take action: '*Uxorius, effeminatus*', you are behaving like a woman. 'In fact, they said that Rollo had never known her according to the law of marriage.' Rollo then broke with the king of the Franks, his father-in-law. The peace was over. The 'pledge' had no further use. Gisla was left to die, probably still a virgin. The anonymous wife of William Longsword is only a shadow. It seems possible that her husband, who despised women, never slept with her. Richard certainly slept with Emma, and, if we are to believe the eulogy of her composed by the canon of Saint-Quentin, it was worth his while. But he was unable to have a child by her. She died, and it was her brother, Hugh Capet, who distributed between churches and the poor all she possessed 'by feminine right', necklaces, bracelets, rings and brooches, diadems, long gowns and copes: the woman's portion, what belonged to them personally, and what the spread of Christianity now prevented from being placed alongside their body in the tomb, as had happened in the past.

4

Mistresses

T he first dukes, nevertheless, were all succeeded by
sons. They produced male children, but by a mistress,
not by their legitimate wife. This was a source of
some embarrassment to the authors who wrote in their
praise. The monk Raoul Glaber, a contemporary of William
the Conqueror, spoke effusively of their virtues. They had
supported his patron, William of Volpiano, who had
reformed the Norman monasteries. Raoul did not, however,
conceal the fact that all these princes had been born of
women he called concubines. But his readers should not be
too shocked by this; had not the patriarchs of the Old
Testament also been polygamous? Dudo had a more difficult
task. The history that he was commissioned to write was
that of a continuous progress towards civilization, and this
progress was inseparable from the spread of Christian morality. It assumed on the part of the leaders of the Norman
people a gradual rejection of the sexual behaviour condemned by the ecclesiastical authorities. In fact, the 'concubines', the mothers of the princes, had themselves contributed
to this progress – the mother of William Longsword, in
particular, who, according to the lament, had baptized her
son in secret. Dudo's book was primarily the story of a
lineage. He could hardly ignore the women who had assured
its continuation, the mother of his sponsor, Richard I, for

example, or the mother of Richard II, who was still alive and venerated at court. So Dudo pitched in.

Without embarrassment, he reported that Richard I, 'driven by the goads of male desire, fathered by concubines two sons and some daughters [how many is not specified]'. He leaves us in no doubt that, in the late tenth century, the leaders of the 'pirates' disported themselves without shame among a troop of women they kept in their house. This sexual activity bore fruit, and many children were born. Dudo thought it necessary only to point out that the duke, once Emma had died, was a widower. This was an excuse. He says nothing about his partners in pleasure, since the two sons born of these illicit unions had not inherited the duchy. Of the beautiful mistresses enjoyed by these princes, only one is mentioned: the woman who had given birth to the successor. This was the boy whom the duke, in the evening of his life, chose from among his assembled male offspring, and, one feast day, presented to the great men of the province, saying, it is he, acclaim him, in the hope that the whole of the nobility, now bound by oath, would recognize as their future guide the son he had chosen.

In a few words, the mother of William Longsword is very precisely located. Rollo, wrote Dudo, 'took with him for his pleasure a certain Poppa, a virgin, beautiful, born of a glorious blood, daughter of the prince Berenger; he bound himself to her by marriage and had by her a son named William.' She was a Frank, she was a Christian and there had been a marriage: *connubium*. William of Jumièges repeated and amplified this passage: 'In Bayeux, the duke seized a young maiden named Poppa, daughter of Berenger, an illustrious man [he was count of Nantes or of Rennes] and soon after he joined himself to her in the Danish manner (*more danico*)'. A monk, William balked at the word *connubium*, and amended it to 'joining together'. By his day, the forms of conjugal union that the Church was endeavouring to impose on the aristocracy had become more clearly defined and stricter. It was now necessary to make sure that the alliance referred to by Dudo was confused neither with Christian marriage nor with simple concubinage. What then was he to say? Rollo and his companions were Vikings; they married in their own fashion, according to their customs and laws. But they married in an orderly way; the days of unregulated promiscuity had passed. Let us allow these foreigners, these immigrants, their own customs, reprehensible, admittedly, but which, as they had become more civilized, they had happily since abandoned. The 'Danish manner' was a memory from a past era, an ethnographic curiosity. William of Jumièges also tells us that Poppa was a prisoner, abducted from a city during the course of looting, the leader's share of the booty brought back from Neustria by the band commanded by Rollo, then settled in England. In fact, this girl was carried across the Channel; the lament specifies that Duke William was born in England. She had been taken and made pregnant, therefore, before the peace and before the marriage to Gisla. The *Deeds of the Norman Dukes* also claims that, after Gisla's death, Rollo recalled Poppa and restored her to his bed, and that he had previously repudiated her; had she ever, one wonders, left his harem? It must not be thought that the first duke, who had been baptized, had had two wives at the same time. But by supposing a repudiation, this account inadvertently established that the union 'in the Danish manner', as William put it, was indeed a true marriage.

Whether it had been a marriage or not was of little interest to the writers who retold and rewrote this story for Henry Plantagenet. For them, it was simply love. 'Rollo,' says Wace, 'who had long desired her, made her his mistress' and, once Gisla was dead, 'he married her and kept her for a long time': a story of desire contained for a while, then amorous conquest, afterwards love and finally marriage. There was nothing here to shock courtly society at the time when Chrétien de Troyes was writing *Cligès*. As for Benoît de Sainte-Maure, he refined, as was his custom, lingering over his description of the charms to which Rollo had succumbed – the face, the throat, 'everything that her robe allowed to be seen and touched'. The duke took her for his wife 'according to the customs of Denmark', then relinquished her, despite himself:

for the daughter of the king of France.
But he did not forget
the great love he had felt for her.

Dudo named neither the woman made pregnant by William Longsword nor his wife, even though she was the mother of Richard, who was his benefactor, and of Raoul of Ivry, who had been his informant. We see here very clearly just how little women mattered. This woman appears only as a foil in poems lauding her son. In connection with his birth, she is said to be not only 'holy', and 'born of a brilliant and free blood', but a 'very dear wife', and when Dudo shows William, 'impelled not by human frailty but by the just desire to assure the succession', resigning himself to a union, he specifies that the chosen partner was, as she should be, a noble virgin, and very spirited. These were stock formulas. What is remarkable, on the other hand, is this cautious clause: the union took place *geniali* (not *maritali*) *jure*; it was not a marriage, but liberty and pleasure. Here, too, William of Jumièges is slightly more informative. The 'most noble maiden' William set out to impregnate was called Sprota. He had married her in the Danish manner, admittedly, but according to the rules. Nevertheless, when the King of the Franks occupied Normandy and entertained the young Richard in his palace at Rouen, he liked to humiliate him by calling him the son of a whore, a hussy wicked enough to have stolen another woman's husband.

At this point, Robert of Torigny adds a note concerning Raoul of Ivry. With William dead and his son Richard in exile in France, Sprota was 'obliged by necessity', he says, 'to share the bed of a very rich man', a *rentier*, farmer of some mills on the River Risle. There was no marriage in this case either, but '*contubernio ... adhesit*', in fact a mixture. 'By this man she had Raoul and also some daughters who were legitimately married to noblemen.' This passage throws light on the birth of Dudo's informant, and on the blood tie that bound him to Duke Richard: they had been born of the same mother. At this point, Robert inserts an account of one of those episodes which so delighted a twelfth-century audience.

The young bastard lived wild in the woods. His half-brother came there to hunt. The hunting party flushed out an enormous bear, before which they fled. Raoul confronted the bear single-handedly and killed it. When he heard of this feat, Richard gave him the forest and the castle of Ivry, and also a woman, who was 'very beautiful', like all the mistresses of princes at the point when they desired and took them. The story is typical of those told within families regarding the founders of lineages: a feat in the forest, its reward, the simultaneous grant of land and a wife. By his own wife, Raoul had two sons who both became bishops, so were without legitimate children. The prior of Bec's interpolation sheds light on the lot of women married 'in the Danish manner'. Once their husband was dead, they passed into the arms of whoever wished to take them. But this was surely also the case, if they were not too worn out, with the women the Church regarded as real wives, for example Anne of Kiev, the widow of King Henry of France, who was seized by a baron as soon as she became available.

In Dudo's book, only one woman really emerges from obscurity. This is the mother of Richard II, one of the women to whom the previous duke bound himself (*se connexit*: a connection, a fortuitous union) when, after the death of his wife, Emma the Frank, he took his pleasure where he chose. He bound himself, says Dudo, 'to a virgin of great dignity', born of a very famous Danish noble family. She was called Gonnor, and she was the most beautiful of all the Norse virgins. He took her *amicabiliter*. This Latin word hints at a romance word, *amie*, the word used in the vocabulary of the courts for the women with whom one amused oneself, the woman whom the lover pretended to treat as his 'lady', when she was not his wife and when the conventions of the game of courtly love precluded her from being his wife. Dudo does not claim that there had been a contract or a marriage, even in the Scandinavian manner. The facts are clear: to begin with, Gonnor was part of the pool in which the prince fished for his partners in pleasure. But the great men of Normandy, 'knowing her to be born of the very noble seed of a glorious family', and uneasy, like the companions of Rollo and

William before them, at the sterility of the official marriage, urged the duke: 'By the providence of God [they took it for granted that Heaven looked kindly on these amorous activities], you have joined yourself to this Norsewoman for whom you burn [fire, promising because favourable to generation]. So that the heir to this land will be born of a Danish father and mother [with integration almost complete, the great men of the duchy were the more anxious to establish their ethnic singularity vis à vis the Franks and by no means displeased to see an extra dose of Scandinavian blood introduced into the ducal lineage], bind yourself to her quickly by the indissoluble tie of the matrimonial pact so that after your death, which draws near, the soil of your duchy will be ruled by a valorous offspring.' Richard took this advice. He married Gonnor 'by [this time] marital law before the bishops and the clergy, the great men and the people'. His aberrations as a widower now in the past, he regularized his liaison and settled down.

William of Jumièges firmly distanced himself from what he found in Dudo. He summarizes, mentions the concubines only after having spoken of Gonnor, says nothing of previous love affairs and records a marriage (*matrimonium*) in the Christian manner (*cristiano more*). This was not enough for Robert of Torigny. Whilst he struggled to reconstitute the genealogy of a descendant of Gonnor, Roger de Montgomery, he added the following story, based on what old men had told him about this woman and her marriage. It was rumoured that the custodian of the forest of Arques had a magnificent wife, a morsel fit for a king. Tempted, Richard went to see for himself. 'Given shelter in the house of the forester, seduced by the beauty of his wife's face [for the moment, all he could see], he demanded that his host bring her to his bed that night. Sadly, the forester went to tell her. She, like a good wife, consoled him, advising him to *supponere*, to "put under", the duke in her place her sister Gonnor, a virgin and more alluring than she was.' This is what they did. 'When he learned of the trick, the duke rejoiced that he had avoided the sin of taking the wife of another.' (For the monk of Bec, adultery was a sin, but in the case of a man without a wife, as the duke then was, random fornication was only a peccadillo.) According to this story, Gonnor, though certainly Scandinavian, came from a less distinguished background than is claimed by Dudo. Richard was not parted from her; he took her with him and cherished her, and the relationship lasted: he had three sons and three daughters by her. When he wanted to make Robert, one of his sons, archbishop of Rouen, canon law prevented him. Robert's mother had not been properly married (*desponsata*). 'It was then that Richard attached her to him in the Christian manner and his sons already born of her were covered by the pall (*pallium*)', the veil that was held over the man and the woman during the nuptial blessings. By this rite, they were legitimized.

A few years later, the poets employed by Henry Plantagenet celebrated the love between Robert and Gonnor. Acclaiming the latter's merits, Wace emphasizes qualities that Dudo attributed to the legitimate wives of the first dukes. 'Of women's work', he said, 'she knew as much as a woman can know.' He was thinking of work with the hands, of embroidery and needlework, but he was surely also – since in his day a high value was placed on girls who knew how to massage (*tastonner*) knights agreeably when they removed their hauberk, and stroke them with expert hands – thinking of the subtle acts which prepared men for love. I find Wace interesting also because, again drawing on the memories of Richard I still preserved by members of the household, he describes the wedding night. 'The night after he married her', the duke saw Gonnor lie down 'in another manner and in another way' than was her habit. She turned her back on him. He was amazed:

> You used to turn your face towards me.
> When, she replied, I slept in your bed
> I submitted to your pleasure. Now I am in my own.
> I will sleep on whatever side I please.
> Before, this bed was yours
> Today, it is mine and yours
> Never have I slept there at ease
> Nor without fear lain down with you.

We see what changed when a mistress became a wife. She ceased to feel simply an object, subject to the wishes of the male, a docile doll in his hands. Her fear disappeared; she was no longer so terrified of sinning. Marriage was this assurance, a right won in bed, the bed of which the wife was now the mistress, a partner there in her own right. This was what, in fact, was being claimed at the time Wace was writing by certain theologians. Had not Abelard declared that in the conjugal bed the two sexes met in parity as on the day of creation? And the wife enjoyed another advantage over the *amie*; she, too, might determine positions.

Dudo of Saint-Quentin, obliged to mention these women who were never, or only tardily, true wives, but who slept with the prince and prevailed over other mistresses by giving him the heir to his power, still spoke cautiously of that aspect of the 'ways of life' it was his job to describe: the polygamy that persisted in his day. Freer than he was, the Frankish historians, Flodoard or Richer, saw the mothers Dudo lauded as women of little importance; for them, Richard was simply born 'of a Breton concubine'. Dudo hedged, using with regard to these liaisons words like 'connection' or 'union'. He was careful not to mention the offensive remarks addressed by Louis d'Outremer to the young Richard, and his account remains vague and brief, except in the case of the mistress of his patron and benefactor, who, he said, 'adorned churches not women'. In fact, Gonnor was still living in the palace, where she held court. And since, on the death of Richard I, the son of another concubine had taken up arms and claimed the inheritance, Dudo insisted on the legitimacy of a union that he regarded as 'prohibited' and culpable, but which ceased to be so as soon as the prescribed rites had taken place and the couple had been placed under 'marital law'. He does not say, we should note, that it was a Christian marriage. What mattered was that these rites and this law had made Gonnor the *uxor*, the wife, and her eldest son the indisputable successor.

William of Jumièges was writing in a monastery. The culture with which he was imbued exalted virginity and demanded chastity of the laity – that is, a sexuality regulated by austere precepts, those, only slightly relaxed, of monasticism; at the time that William was summarizing and amending the work of Dudo, the prelates were endeavouring to impose this same morality. The reform which is called Gregorian was in full swing in Normandy. The councils were laying down the rules of good marriage, whilst the bishops and zealots for purity were inveighing against the wives of priests, demanding that they be cast out: they were not properly married, they were concubines, a word which, in their mouth, meant simply whore. For the honour of the princely line, it was therefore important that no one could confuse the female forebears, the mothers of successive dukes, with these loose women, but that they should be seen as lawfully joined to the father of their son. This is why the monk of Jumièges refers to exotic matrimonial customs, not Christian and therefore imperfect, but nevertheless instituting procreation within the rules. Was it he who invented the concept of 'marriage in the Danish manner', for the good of the cause? We may suspect, at least, that it originated in the entourage of William the Conqueror, in order to justify after the event the rights of those sons who, like him, were chosen by their father to succeed him from amongst all the sons produced by their many mistresses, at a time when the ecclesiastical conception of conjugality was taking shape, when the Christian ritual of marriage was being established and when, simultaneously, the notion of a bastardy that deprived of the right to inherit was being formulated.

A few decades later, Robert of Torigny, also a monk but less remote than William from the lay aristocracy and its culture, disclosed a little of matters about which his predecessors had kept silent: the indulgence of their family towards the sexual conduct of the princes, and those excesses that the family imagination liked to transfer to deep in the woods, to the realm of dreams, caprice and play. In this, Robert was the precursor of Wace and Benoît. Both were clerics, but nevertheless fully integrated into the courtly society to whose tastes they pandered and whose thoughts and longings they did their best to express. They returned unhesitatingly to

Dudo. They were not interested in whether carnal relations
between men and women who were the ancestors of their
protectors had taken place within the context of a proper
marriage or in lustful aberrations. They emphasized love,
love as it was played out before their eyes and as it was made
in the fashionable world. They now opposed the mistress,
not the whore, to the wife. Far from shocking them, the
polygamy of former times intrigued them and they viewed it
indulgently, just as they viewed the polygamy of their contemporaries, the philandering knights, indulgently. Among
the men with whom they were familiar, 'very rare, in fact,
are those who are content with only one woman'. These
were the words of the chronicler Gislebert, canon of Mons,
and they thought the same, and from experience. Like those
who enjoyed their poems, they demanded only that the rules
of the game – that strict code within which it was permitted,
without muddle, outside marriage, to indulge in the pleasures
of amorous contests – were not broken. In the imagination
of Wace and Benoît, the first princes of Normandy treated
women as it was prescribed that they should be treated by
the laws of that game which the historians of medieval
literature have called courtly love, laws promulgated in order
to contain and control male sexual exuberance. For these
writers, as for all who listened to them, this virile ardour was
a virtue. It was natural that it should be given free rein
outside the confines of marriage. All that mattered was that
honour was safeguarded. *Fin'amor* replaced the 'commune'
of savage times with 'decent customs', precise rules for the
pursuit of women. The writers who worked for Henry
Plantagenet, consequently, fitted the attitudes of Rollo and
of Richard into the complex amorous intrigues of the *Roman
de Troie*. The customs of the court required this cover, in
practice a very light and transparent veil, through which the
reality – the substance, the appetite for enjoying and savour-
ing the pleasures of the body – was clearly visible. These
pleasures had already been discreetly hinted at by Dudo of
Saint-Quentin, when he chose to describe the prolific couplings of his heroes with an extremely rare adjective, *fescenni-
nus* (one would like to know by which Romance words the

'reading clerks' translated this for the benefit of their audience), in no way condemning these pleasures, but rather praising the partners of the former dukes, wives or not, for having known how to please them by the attractions of their flesh, by their willingness and by their dexterity.

5

Arlette

William of Jumièges, Wace and Benoît all mention
the birth of Duke William, who was for a long
time surnamed the Bastard. His father, Robert,
son of Richard II, was, apart from his brother, the only one
of the first seven dukes of Normandy who was the product
of a legitimate marriage. He was called the Devil on account
of the blackness of his soul, but also the Magnificent because
he displayed great generosity and brimmed over with vitality.
He died 'young', that is to say without having married, on
2 July 1035, at Nicaea in Asia Minor, while on a pilgrimage
to Jerusalem. He had gone there to cleanse himself of his
sins. He had probably poisoned his brother, Richard III,
whom their father had designated to succeed him at the head
of the duchy. To appease his ambitions, Robert had been
given the county of Hiemois, round the castle of Falaise. But
he was not satisfied. 'Badly advised', he rebelled, and fought
a hard war. Peace was eventually made. Duke Richard and
Robert shook each other by the right hand, then sat down to
eat together as a sign of reconciliation. Hardly had the duke
returned to his palace in Rouen when he was seized with
stomach pains and died. Everybody spoke of poison. William
of Jumièges spoke of it, too, on the basis of 'what many
people said'. There was no reason why he should keep quiet.
Robert had died at peace, as white as snow. To die on the

hard road to the Holy Land earned remission of the gravest sins. Before setting off, Robert had arranged his succession, as pilgrims did. In a manner similar to that described by Dudo, he had presented the young William to his barons, 'this only son that he had fathered at Falaise', asking them to make him 'prince of the militia at the head of the Norman knights'. Everything went well, and according to the *Deeds of the Norman Dukes*, the great men of the country gladly gave their agreement and swore the oath of loyalty. Robert set out, never to return.

William of Jumièges wrote in the Conqueror's lifetime, and left it at that. Wace, when reconstructing the scene, projected into the past the customs of his own day and shows Robert leading his son to the king of France, presenting him 'by the fist', so that the young William should become his man and be invested with the duchy in due form. Wace then makes him speak these important words: 'I recognize and take him for mine.' The affirmation of paternity was in fact extremely useful. There is ample evidence that, in the great houses of this period, women were inadequately protected from male assaults. Were the many women the duke slept with as well protected as his lady and wife? Who could swear that the duke was the only man to have made them pregnant? Benoît de Sainte-Maure makes him say 'He is mine, and this is not in doubt' and specify,

> This son that I had of the young woman.
> Though he is not of a wife, do not let this worry you.

In fact, some of the war leaders who wanted to profit from William's minority to extend their powers at his expense claimed that he was not the duke's son. *Nothus* is how William of Jumièges translated into Latin the word bastard, the word that Roger of Tosny, a descendent of the father of Rollo, hurled contemptuously in William's face, and the word that was repeated by Conan, the count of the Bretons, who claimed the whole inheritance: 'You seized Normandy against the law since you are a bastard.' Both of them questioned not the legitimacy of the union which had produced William, but the formula of recognition solemnly pronounced by Robert the Devil, 'who', added Conan, 'you think is your father'. William of Jumièges, obviously, rejected such claims. It remained the fact, nevertheless, undeniable and embarrassing, and justifying the accusation of bastardy, hence the political challenge, that William had been born outside marriage and of a mother one was entitled to despise. Information about the status of this woman comes from the monks who completed the *Deeds of the Norman Dukes* at the beginning of the twelfth century, in particular Orderic Vitalis.

Orderic reveals that she was generally believed to be of humble origins. When William was besieging Alençon, he said, the townspeople taunted him by waving skins and hides from the top of the ramparts, under his very nose, to remind him that 'his mother's family were tanners'. He is more specific when he comments on the insult levelled by Roger of Tosny, *nothus*. It was true that William was a bastard: 'he was born of a concubine of Duke Robert called Herleva, daughter of his chamberlain, Fulbert'. So she was the daughter not of a tanner but of a household servant. Herleva was one of those girls born of servants and raised in the master's household from whom the latter chose his mistresses. The father of her son never took her as his wife. Concubine, the word chosen to describe her, ranks her with the 'wives' of the priests, those sinful illicit mistresses who, according to the reforming prelates of this period, should be thrown out into the streets. Orderic tells us, lastly, that Herleva, after the death of Duke Robert, was taken, this time as legitimate wife, by a knight of good birth, Herluin, to whom she gave two sons, 'Odo and Robert, later very famous'. The mistress of Robert the Magnificent fared rather better, then, than the mistress of William Longsword. She became a proper wife, and the children of her second marriage, like those of Sprota, were the loyal and dearly loved companions of their elder brother.

Accused of bastardy by the Norman nobility, and especially by 'those born of the race of Richard', William had to fight a hard battle against many rivals, against the descendants of the first companions of Rollo and the descendants of the sisters of Gonnor, against the men of his blood, above all, men born either of another of his father's concubines or of a mistress of his grandfather, and against, lastly, his closest cousins, of impeccably legitimate birth, who were the most dangerous of all. It needed a judgement of God, one of those fierce, pitched battles, one of those rare and solemn military liturgies by which, in a day, as at Hastings or Bouvines, the fate of a state was settled at one go, before William was assured of peaceful possession of Normandy: Heaven designated the legitimate pretender by awarding him the victory in 1047, twelve years after the death of his father, at the battle of the Val des Dunes.

The polygamy of the princes here reveals its downside, as a dangerous factor for discord. We see also how much the shaping of Christian marriage, the definition of concubinage and of bastardy and the establishment of firm family structures based on primogeniture, during the first half of the eleventh century, contributed to the institution of a new political order after the year 1000. Previously, the risks of conflict had been averted by the authority of the head of the house and by a ceremonial of collective recognition and approbation. When he had no son born of a wife, it was accepted that the prince would choose from among the boys swarming at his knees and designate the one who would inherit his power, and in so doing elevate above the others one of his mistresses. On the death of Robert the Magnificent, these procedures of legitimation failed in their purpose for three reasons: first, because the orphan was a minor; second, because lordships based on castles were being created throughout the province and the emergence of what we call feudalism was undermining ducal power; and third, because the ecclesiastical conception of marriage was beginning to prevail, condemning all other forms of procreation as illegal, and, with the battle for the celibacy of the clergy raging, the mistresses of princes were being likened to the wives of priests, and their sons to the sons of priests, who were now being denied the right to succeed their father in the priesthood. In fact, Herleva occupied a position very similar to that

of the mistresses of the earlier dukes, those women William
of Jumièges described as wives in the Danish manner. Her
liaison with Robert was not just a passing fancy; it lasted,
and a second child, Adelaide, was born, who was taken as
wife without reluctance by the count of Mons. But Duke
Robert had no intention of binding himself more closely,
whatever her charms, to the daughter of his valet, who was
probably of servile status, like most household servants at
this period. Robert the Devil was well aware that bigamy was
no longer an option. He intended to remain free to make, one
day, an official and political marriage to a woman of a blood
equal to his own, worthy of him, a first cousin of a king of
England. But he died too soon and everyone – William of
Jumièges, Orderic Vitalis and Robert of Torigny – regarded
as a bastard the boy who, as a precaution, and provisionally,
the duke had appointed before his departure as his heir
presumptive. Nevertheless, the son of Herleva defeated the
rebels, with the aid of his two half-brothers. He married,
subsequently presenting himself as the defender of good
morals, and his double victory, at the Val des Dunes and then
at Hastings, confirmed in the eyes of all around him that God
saw him as the legitimate leader of the ducal house.

A century after his death, to please his great-grandson
Henry Plantagenet, Wace and Benoît de Sainte-Maure constructed a beautiful amorous episode on the basis of a few
words written by Orderic in the margin of the *Deeds of the
Norman Dukes*. Wace places the adventure with several
others which testify to the 'magnificence' of Duke Robert.
Benoît expands the story, and it is thanks to him that we can
see how people in court circles liked to imagine relationships
of free love. In his exuberant youth, the duke chased girls
relentlessly. 'It was one of his favourite sports', said Benoît,
'to have girls.' One of them attracted his attention as he
passed. Close to a spring, with other laundresses, she was
washing the household linen. This was women's work, she
was 'a daughter of the town'. It was hot, and Arlot, or Arlette
– the name has stayed with her in history, so let us keep it –
had hitched up her gown, revealing beauties normally con-
cealed: her tantalizing legs. Robert saw them, 'beautiful and

white'. He 'turned his love towards the girl', by which we should understand that he wanted to sleep with her.

The portrait of Arlette sketched by Benoît de Sainte-Maure is disappointing. He banally endows this daughter of the people with all the attractions customarily attributed to princesses: wisdom, courtesy, prowess and beauty. Her hair was fair, her forehead smooth, her eyes without pride, her mouth perfect, as were her chin, her neck and her arms. He says nothing of the soft white regions which were decently covered by the clothes of respectable girls, one glimpse of which was enough to kindle in Robert the Devil, in the very depths of his being, the fever of desire. Three adjectives, lastly, summarize the attractions of Arlette: she was 'lovely', she was 'white' and she was 'plump'.

The smitten duke sent two men of his household, an old knight and his private chamberlain, to speak to the girl's father. Let him agree to allow the prince 'to love' his daughter 'with a great love'; when the duke was tired of her, he would marry her off to some rich lord. But the father refused; he planned to give his daughter in marriage to the man he would choose himself, in consultation with his family. She was already in demand, from several quarters. He did not want to see her, while he was alive, 'pandering to any man' to serve male lust. It is at this point that the person whose function in courtly romances was to articulate chivalric morality, the hermit, made his appearance. He was a brother of the father and a holy man. He persuaded him to give his consent; he also persuaded his niece, reminding her of all the advantages the encounter promised for her. Agreement was reached, and the time when the precious object was to be handed over was settled; it was to be at night, obviously, time of guilty pleasures.

The maiden then declared herself 'terrified', not of being taken, but of not appearing sufficiently attractive to the man who was going to take her. She prepared herself:

> She made a new dress,
> Beautiful, well cut and very seemly,
> And very becoming to her body.

It was the setting for the precious jewel she was to give. When the day came, at the agreed time, the two emissaries arrived. They had orders to take Arlette to the castle secretly, so that the deed would not be known or gossiped about by the 'common people'. This was less for the honour of the prince, whose affairs were viewed indulgently by the people, than for that of the young girl. So the messengers were going to wrap Arlette up in the woollen blanket they had brought with them. Once the deed was done, they would bring her back home, before the lark sang. No one would see or know anything about it. At these words, Arlette objected, stubbornly refusing the secrecy; since the duke had sent for her, 'since he asked for her lovely body', he was not going to take her in passing as if she were a chambermaid. She demanded an escort, and claimed a palfrey like married women had. Then, further enhancing the charms of her appearance, she dressed herself like a fiancée, with a shift of fine cloth and, over it, a pelisse of white, fresh, squirrel fur, without laces, close-fitting, especially around the arms, and a short mantle, and she bound her hair with a silver chain. She did not wear a wimple; she was still a virgin, so her hair would blow in the wind like that of the girls who were led to the chamber of their husband. On the doorstep, she took leave of her father and mother. She wept, as custom required, but her heart was glad, because she knew that she was going to become pregnant that very night, and that the boy that she would carry, more glorious than Hector, would surpass Arthur and Charlemagne. It was the sin that she dreaded. By taking the virginity of a girl he did not intend to marry, the duke, that night, would sin. Not against sexual morality; he was young and he was unmarried, and that he should enjoy himself sleeping with girls was in the nature of things. He would sin against social morality, because he was about to have sex in order to father a hero, and an act as serious as this should not be performed in secrecy. So Arlette refused to slip furtively into the castle by a side door. She wanted a solemn entry, like one about to become a wife.

It is in the 'painted chamber', adorned, like the alabaster

chamber in the *Roman de Troie*, for the pleasures of love, that Wace situates the piquant and marvellous heart of the story. Arlette got into bed, still wearing her shift. To Robert's surprise, with one sweeping gesture, she tore it open at the front, ripping it right down to her feet. It would not be decent, she said, for the hem of this garment, having touched her feet and her legs, to be turned, as she pulled it up, towards the mouth of such a noble lover. These words spoken in bed by a woman matched those of Gonnor. But the bed in which Arlette was taking her place was not a marriage bed, it was not 'hers'. By solemnly baring herself, she was proclaiming her surrender, in total reverence, to that male body whose semen she was about to receive. Benoît de Sainte-Maure ventures a little further. He describes the young woman undressing bit by bit, removing first her sleeves, then, one by one, exposing her charms.

> The candle burned brightly,
> the body looked very well proportioned.

All happened in the light, not shamefully, in the obscurity preferred by fornicators. It was an exposition, of this body proudly offered to the man who was about to take it, and it was the most beautiful he had ever seen. What did he then do with it? Benoît is discreet: 'I wish to say no more.'

It was left to the imagination. Afterwards, Arlette slept. As often happens to the mother of the hero in the lives of saints, and as happened to St Ida of Boulogne before she carried in her womb the future Godfrey de Bouillon, Arlette had a dream. She saw a tree growing out of her belly, that thick and many-branched tree which, when full grown, would give its shade to the whole of Normandy. In fact, she had already conceived; she had, according to Benoît de Sainte-Maure, 'made good use of her virginity'. Wace concludes with the childhood of William. His father

> brought him up lavishly
> and just as nobly
> as if he was born of a wife.

It was clear that Henry Plantagenet had no need to blush for his great-grandmother. Her family may have been from the town, but she was 'wise and valiant', and she had played her role perfectly, making sure that the sexual act was honoured and the wedding ritual respected: her parents had consented and allowed her to go; appropriately adorned, she had been led in procession to the sacrificial altar. What is more, she had proved immediately fertile, ready to be insem- inated, as the priests required and as it was hoped, in court circles, that all wives would be. Nothing was lacking, except for daylight, the banquet and public rejoicings, and except, above all, for the blessings of the Church. But God at least, it appeared, had blessed the union and its fruit, the God of the hermits, pretty tolerant with regard to carnal pleasures. Arlette had trusted him, 'that he would give her fertile joy'. God had not turned away, legitimating William from his conception, exculpating him by his special grace from an apparent bastardy.

Part III

The Power of Women

To a duke of Normandy, the lord of Ardres and even the count of Guînes were pretty small beer. Like Henry Plantagenet, however, they set out, in 1194, to erect a literary monument to their ancestors. Of all the family histories which preserve traces of the women of that period, theirs is without doubt the richest and the raciest. By chance, we can read it still. The land of Guînes, located on the line which separated the warring kings of France and England, occupied a position of great strategic and political importance during the Hundred Years War and after; it was coveted, divided and reconquered. It was here, between Guînes and Ardres, that was held, from 7–24 June 1520, the famous Field of the Cloth of Gold, at which Francis I and Henry VIII competed in magnificence. Further, the county passed to illustrious houses, close to the monarchy: the Brienne acquired it from the king of France who had bought it in 1282; it then passed to the house of Bar, one of the offshoots of the house of Bourbon. In these great houses, a document which told of distant ancestors and of a disputed inheritance was looked after with care. It was copied and recopied and it was translated into Latin. The oldest surviving manuscript is found in the Vatican library (number 696) in the collection bequeathed by Queen Christina of Sweden. It is a beautifully produced book, whose writing has been dated to the fifteenth century.

The first of the 123 folios of this book is missing. It is likely that it presented, as frontispiece, an illustration. From another copy, which the *bailli* and the schoolmaster of the little town of Audruicq checked with the original in 1586, we know that three coats of arms appeared on this page: on the one hand, the arms of France and on the other, quartered, those of the counts of Guînes and the lords of Ardres. Below, there appeared a seated prince receiving a book from the hands of a man, who was standing and wearing a long gown. This double image perfectly defined the nature of the work. It was the history of two different houses, Guînes and Ardres, separate since their origins but recently united by marriage; both were subject to the authority of the king of France, but Ardres was subordinate to Guînes. Its author, who hands over the manuscript to the man who had commissioned him to write it, is a man of the Church, a 'master'. He gives his name, Lambert, in the first line, in the title of the prologue, and describes himself soon after as 'priest of the church of Ardres'.

The 1586 copy has disappeared, but it was copied many times. From it derive the modern editions which give easy access to this fascinating document. Fascinating, because it is, in the full sense of the word, extraordinary – so racy, so graphic and so natural, providing so much concrete information about the most basic facts of everyday life, that it has disconcerted scholars. In addition, since the earliest copies of it to survive postdate it by more than three centuries, its authenticity has been questioned. What we read must surely, it is said, have been forged at the end of the Middle Ages. This hypothesis, as F. L. Ganshof has so skilfully shown, does not hold up; no forger could so successfully have appropriated the attitudes and world-view, or so convincingly have imitated the way of writing, of a contemporary of Philip Augustus. Once assured of the veracity of this document, historians of feudal society have seized on it, Marc Bloch in particular, after Guilhermoz. I have used it myself on many occasions, though I have been very far from exploiting all its riches. I return to this history now for what it reveals about the power of women.

1

The Context

O ne of the merits of this book, the chief one perhaps
for my purposes, is that it describes the milieu in
which the dozen or so women whom Lambert had
known and seen with his own eyes had lived, and in which,
unconcerned for anachronism, he placed the other women,
whose names were repeated within the family and about
whom his patron expected him to speak though they were
now dead, some of them for centuries. Of course, these
women are lost among a host of men, overwhelmed and
stifled by them. This history, too, is a history of warriors. In
the prologue and the preface, the author proclaims this
loudly. He had embarked on the book at the request of a
man, 'the very valiant knight . . . Arnold of Guînes . . . his
lord and his master'. He wrote 'in praise of, to the glory of
and in honour of' the ancestors of this Arnold, so that the
memory 'of their name and of their deeds' would be preserved; these ancestors were men, 'the counts of Guînes and
the great men of Ardres'. Behind these male figures, gesticu-
lating, posturing, swaggering about in the foreground, one
spies, now and again, the figure of a woman. She disappears
almost at once. The most the historian can do is sometimes
catch a fleeting glimpse of a few features. We do not find
here, as in the history of the lords of Amboise or in that of
the dukes of Normandy, even the sketchiest portrait of a

woman. We have only a few words of praise, here and there, and Lambert employs the same formulas whether he is speaking of the mistress of the house or of one of the young women that her husband pursued and seduced in passing. They were all, without exception, described as 'noble' and 'beautiful' – no more, no less. We have to accept that it is those most valiant of knights who occupy centre stage; they expected the narrator to proclaim their virtues. What purpose would be served by talking about women? They counted for so little. This is one of the most striking lessons taught by this narrative. It is not, however, altogether a bad thing that the men should be there, and so vividly portrayed. It is essential, clearly, to allow them their place; otherwise, we risk misconceiving the status, the rights and the duties of the women. History has for too long been written without regard for women, but we must not therefore fall into the opposite trap, of conceiving a history of women which pays no attention to men. In the twelfth century as today, men and women did not exist in isolation. What I hope my enquiry will achieve is a better understanding of the relations between the two sexes.

The setting is male and therefore military. The ladies of Guînes and the ladies of Ardres all had for husband a man who was a mighty warrior, master of a fortress he firmly believed had been built by his most distant ancestor, founder of the dynasty. Lambert believed this, too. For him, each of these two lineages had originated at the same time as a castle, when the leader of a band of mounted men decided 'to raise firstly a great mound of earth to make a fort [what Romance dialects of this period called a motte], then to surround it with a double ditch'. These are the words used to describe the beginnings of the castle of Guînes, which was certainly built first. Whether this was in the first decades of the tenth century, as Lambert assumed, is doubtful. Wishing to push the origins of this lineage far back into the past, Lambert started from a few male names which had lingered in the memory. He arbitrarily constructed the first three rungs of the genealogy. In fact, the oldest Guînes attested by archival sources are a Eustace and a Baldwin, two names that attach them to the two most powerful houses in the region, those of the counts of Boulogne and of the counts of Flanders, both proud of their descent from Charlemagne. Eustace lived around 1030. He had apparently been one of the boys maintained by the count of Flanders, who gave him the daughter of his treasurer as wife. It is probable that he bore the title of count. His son Baldwin, at any rate, is given this title in an act subscribed by King Philip I in 1065. The prosperity of the family and, if not the foundation, at least the reinforcement of the castle may well date back to the first two or three decades of the eleventh century; it was at this period that, in northern France, the masters of a few powerful fortresses managed to appropriate the comital dignity, so taking their place among those delegates to whom God, through the intermediary of the king, his lieutenant, had given official responsibility for ensuring that peace reigned on earth in his name.

Lambert was better informed about the castle of Ardres. His patron lived there, he himself had spent his childhood there, and the motte stood next to the church where he was priest. It was firmly believed within the family that the castle had been built around 1050 by Arnold. This Arnold was an adventurer, perhaps a younger son, the great-great-grandfather of the Arnold to whom Lambert dedicated his book. Less than eight kilometres from the castle of Guînes, in a space which was then deserted, 'between two sluices a stone's throw apart, deep in a muddy marsh, not far from the foot of a hill, this Arnold raised a pile of earth, a very high motte or a tower, as a sign of defence'. It was, then, a sign, the emblem of a power to command and to punish, to maintain order by force of arms. Legends surrounded the founding act, on which was based all the honour of the 'great men of Ardres'. A tame bear was supposed to have helped shift the earth, and a little gem embellished with gold, a lucky pendant, had been found hidden in the middle of the motte, 'in an obscure and secret place'. Arnold carved out a place for himself, too, by manoeuvring between the counts of Flanders and those of Boulogne. It was Baldwin V of Flanders who encouraged him to build the castle in order to weaken

the count of Guînes, whose emerging power made him
uneasy. So Arnold became 'sire' and one of the twelve peers
of Flanders. He also served Eustace of Boulogne, the father
of Godfrey de Bouillon, who rewarded him generously by
allowing him to marry the widow of the count of Saint-Pol,
so giving him the means to exploit to his advantage this
prosperous lordship. Lambert says that Arnold devoted what
he earned from this affair to making the castle of Ardres
even grander.

At the same time, he set out to get himself accepted and
integrated into the network of pre-existing powers. He
attached himself first to the ecclesiastical institutions, which
were less demanding, to the bishopric of Thérouanne and to
the abbey of Saint-Bertin, which entrusted to him the task of
ensuring justice and peace throughout its lands. Later, a rich
man, 'he resided in safety in his Ardres', and finally came to
an understanding with the count of Guînes, chief lord of the
territory in which he had settled, getting him to recognize the
complete freedom of the *châtillon*, the little *oppidum* he had
built. Lambert, who saw large quantities of money in circulation around him, and used for every purpose, tells us that,
in return for this franchise, Arnold gave the count 'a barrelful
of pennies'. In 1094, on the eve of his death, he attached
himself more closely to the count of Flanders, accepting back
the keep as a fief from Robert II and doing homage for it.
Nevertheless, the first of the lords of Ardres did not feel that
the protection with which he had surrounded himself, the
ramparts of earth and wood, the ditches, his alliances and
his escort of warriors, were enough. It seemed to him just as
necessary, if not more so, to assure himself of the favours of
heaven, and to surround himself with a team of men of
prayer. He built an *ecclesiola*, a little church dedicated to St
Omer, on the hill above the castle. A priest visited it from
time to time to say an office. One day in 1069, with the
agreement of the bishop and the local priest, Arnold went to
the door of this oratory accompanied by his sons and
daughters. On the threshold, he declared, aloud, before God
and St Omer, that he renounced all power over that place.
He then entered the church and placed on the altar a banner

marked with a cross, sign of the transfer of power, from which hung a green olive branch, sign of peace. He provided a relic enshrined in gold and precious stones, one of St Omer's teeth, which the canons had extracted for him from the head of their patron, and then some books, the Old and New Testaments, and church ornaments. He had taken them from the treasury of the collegiate church of Saint-Pol, of which he was the guardian in the name of his wife. Once properly furnished, the *ecclesiola* could become an *ecclesia*, the centre of a parish. All that was needed was to install a resident priest, and Arnold installed several. He observed that the castles of the count of Flanders and of other local lords all had a collegiate church and a chapter of canons close by. So he created ten prebends, and gave one to the priest in charge and another to one of his bastards, already a canon of Saint-Omer. This college would pray for him and for his subjects. A little later, he moved it to a new building, placed under the patronage of the Holy Virgin. Standing next to his castle, it was 'like his chapel', a private place of worship, where the sire sat among the canons, directed them, sang with them, and ritually distributed alms, as did the count of Flanders, his lord. Thus, Arnold of Ardres sacralized the power that he owed to his arms. To the same end, in 1084, Count Baldwin I of Guînes founded an abbey for men at Andres, near to his castle.

With great intelligence and skill, Lambert drew out the family memory. It is extremely valuable, because it shows how, in the eleventh century, little states grew up around a fortification and a sanctuary. Of the two in question here, one, in principle, dominated the other. Lambert signals this clearly. There were the Ardres, his patrons, whom he calls *proceres*, 'great men', 'leaders'. Whereas the Guînes were counts and, as such, convinced they were entitled to exercise authority over all the inhabitants of the comital territory, including over the lords of the castle of Ardres. When one of the Guînes married his son to an Ardres heiress, he was, says Lambert, demeaned. In practice, the two principalities were of equal strength, doomed to fight each other: Ardres, the more recent, was inserted like a wedge into the other. This is why this history of knights consists essentially, like the courtly romances, of a succession of military incidents. War never ceased for two centuries in the land of Guînes.

Lambert briefly describes this countryside: 'It lends itself to pastoral activities, to the rearing of sheep and other beasts; it is undulating and bosky, dotted with copses; fields alternate with pastures; it is bordered by a wet, marshy plain.' There were, in fact, two adjacent countrysides: the far side of the hills of the Boulonnais, and below them, to the north, a vast plain. In late Antiquity, it had been flooded by the sea. It had then gradually been filled in and settled. In Lambert's day, it was dotted with new parishes, the reclamation was almost complete, and what unclaimed land remained was beginning to be disputed. When the brother of Arnold of Guînes wanted to 'dig up and cut for peat' a stretch of marsh, his neighbours and the commoners rose up against him. Lambert had seen this and, in the last chapter of his book, he tells of a more serious conflict. There still remained, within the offshore bar, a fairly extensive stretch of watery solitude, which was known as the king's marsh. It formed the frontier between the land of Guînes and that of Boulogne. Count Baldwin II set out to drain it. Soon hearing of this, the seneschal of the count of Boulogne summoned the inhabitants of the land of Marck, the 'keurebroeders', the customary fraternity. All – men on foot and men on horseback – were to assemble with thirty days' provisions, their tools and their arms; they were to dig a deep ditch that would protect the land from takeover by the neighbouring lord. So they started to cut down the trees already planted by the count's servants, to dig, to fling earth about, and they mocked the men on the other side. The latter retaliated. From a vantage-point on the top of a hillock, Count Baldwin watched the enemy flee in disarray, knocked about and scattered, 'some on the pathways, others in the ditches, others in the marsh'. His men carried their banners back home and hung them up as tokens of victory in the church of Ardres.

The quarrel was minor, an insignificant episode in the permanent hostility between rival principalities. I record it, nevertheless, because it shows how productive land was becoming scarce in a countryside beginning to fill up as a result of rapid population growth. It shows also that live-stock farming was highly profitable in these hills 'with extensive pastures', and even more so in the salt marshes of the plain. Prosperity came chiefly, however, from the road. Guînes and Ardres were situated on a major axis of circula-tion across Europe, the network of highways connecting up with old Roman roads leading from England via Sangatte, Wissant and other shores towards Saint-Omer, the town which the counts of Flanders had fortified at the gates of the very ancient abbey of Saint-Bertin, and towards Thérouanne, the vestige of a Roman city, in decay, certainly, but not yet obliterated from the map, since the bishop, his chapter and the cathedral school were still there. From Saint-Omer, the road led towards Ypres, Ghent and Bruges, and from Thér-ouanne towards Arras, France and Champagne, and towards Rome. At every period, men of war, pilgrims and traders had travelled this route. For two centuries their numbers had grown and their activities had increased. The rapid develop-ment of a small market town at the gate of the castle of Ardres was a sign of this steady growth of traffic.

People still remembered the time when, close to an old Roman station, now drowned under stagnant waters, there had been only a bar where people went to drink beer. The local peasantry gathered there to *chouler*, that is to play the local ball-game. Strangers stopped there too, especially those Italian traders who, said Lambert, 'went to England on business'. Arnold the founder inevitably chose this spot to build his fortress in the marsh: his warriors would protect the travellers and receive silver coins in return. Hoping that they, too, could share in the profits from the traffic and trade, migrants flocked in from the surrounding villages. A souk, a Thursday market, soon developed under the control of the lord. Around 1100, the agglomeration became a *bourg* when the master of the castle had it enclosed 'with a large ditch, deep and wide'. Sixty years later, courts were held there and merchandise was displayed under the lead roof of a solidly-constructed market hall. The women who appear in this history lived, we should not forget, in one of the parts of

Christendom then most strongly invigorated by the growth of trade. For the lords of the two castles, the count in particular, the road was expensive. He was expected to offer hospitality to travellers of high status. At the beginning of the thirteenth century, people still remembered the lavish receptions accorded several decades earlier to the archbishop of Canterbury, Thomas Becket, and to the archbishop of Reims. On those occasions, white wine had flowed like water in the dining-room. It came from far away, from the vineyards of Laon, or Paris, and it was expensive. But the protectors of the public peace also made lots of money from the road, money that had become so necessary by the time Lambert was completing his history, and indispensable if war was to be waged effectively.

Except on days of heavy rain or wind or harsh winter weather, when they stayed under cover at home, the count of Guînes and the lord of Ardres, clad in hauberk, sword in hand, rode out at the head of their men. War was their profession and their pleasure. For a long time, and as soon as the castle of Ardres was built, they fought against each other, even though the first lord of Ardres had done homage, and in spite of the pile of silver coins he had poured out at the feet of the count to mollify him. One pursued the other as far as the moat of the castle, kept him penned in there for a while, raised the siege when he saw friends of the besieged riding to the rescue, then retreated, with them hot on his heels, driven back in his turn into his own keep. One day, they agreed to kiss and make up. For a while, a truce interrupted these damaging forays. But the plain was ruined and sometimes people were killed. One of the lords of Ardres had his skull pierced by an arrow and nearly died during the course of these antics. After more than a century of skirmishes, the rivalry miraculously ended. By chance succeeding his brother-in-law, who had died during the second crusade, Arnold IV, the new lord of Ardres, wanted peace. He finally made up with Count Arnold. The two Arnolds joined forces to defend the land of Guînes. They were now 'like the two hands of a single body', 'like a single heart, like a single soul', models of vassalic amity. 'Guînes exulted in the peace, and the court of Ardres rejoiced with them ... the count no longer aspired to use his arrogant power with regard to his vassal and subject, who ceased the old rebellion and no longer refused his lord honour and reverence.' A marriage sealed the agreement. Arnold of Ardres gave his daughter and heiress to the elder son of Arnold of Guînes. From this union was born a new Arnold, and it was he who was the patron of Lambert. The main function of the wife, mixing the two seeds, was clearly, as I have said, to consolidate the accord between the house from which she came and the house to which she was led on her wedding day.

The two princelings engaged in many other battles. Each of them, within his own territory, endeavoured to control those malcontents whom Lambert called the 'vavassors', the most powerful of their subjects and their more or less close relations. Well provided with land and slaves, controlling a dozen or more peasant families, sometimes rich enough to found monasteries and chapters of canons, in fact the equals of the count and the sire, these unruly warriors demanded to be treated accordingly. They were prickly, and constantly in revolt. Above all, they dreamed of one day building a keep, like their cousin, the founder of the castle of Ardres, and of creating their own lordship. From time to time, one of these country squires ordered the peasant tenants who owed him labour services to take up their spade and dig, to raise up one of those entrenchments which Lambert describes as dotting the countryside, abandoned because Guînes and Ardres had nipped these rival enterprises in the bud. This had not been achieved without difficulty or without brutality. People still remembered those rebel vassals whom the counts of ancient times had decapitated, or whose genitals they had cut off, laughing as they did so. At the end of the twelfth century, these 'grandees' of the second rank remained turbulent and dangerous. The count tried to hold onto them by giving his nieces in marriage to their sons.

All the lords of Ardres also went further afield to fight, overseas, to England or to the Holy Land. Arnold I and his two recently knighted sons accompanied William the Conqueror in 1066, in the band recruited by Eustace of Boulogne.

They served William for many years and were handsomely rewarded. They received fine estates in Bedfordshire and Cambridgeshire as fiefs and returned home with a large sum of money, and also a bear, a gift from the king, which gave much pleasure to their subjects. Arnold II took the cross in 1095 in response to the appeal of Urban II. In the army led by Robert of Flanders, he took part in the victorious attacks on Antioch and Jerusalem. Baldwin, his son, joined the second crusade, and Arnold, his great-grandson, made preparations to go on the third. The counts, however, travelled less. Only one of the brothers of Manassé followed the first crusades. But Manassé, in his youth, when his father was slow to die, had briefly ventured further afield. Having crossed the Channel, he put his arms in the service of William the Conqueror's son, William Rufus, which earned him a wealthy wife, Emma of Tancarville, daughter of the chamberlain of England.

The Guînes and the Ardres, lastly, all regularly joined in the tournaments that the princes organized all year round in the provinces of France. During these periods of licence, when, for the fun of it, knights enthusiastically traded blows, all the time on the lookout for the chance to capture horses and ransom the vanquished, the two families forgot the inveterate hatred that divided them. On these occasions, the two parties of knights formed one team, the Ardres serving the Guînes, the Guînes behaving 'graciously' towards the Ardres. They 'gladly won honour together'. Throughout his narrative, Lambert refers constantly to tournaments. It is on their vast fields, where, before expert eyes, new knights displayed their courage and their skills in horsemanship, that the priest of Ardres presents, one after the other, the ancestors of the two families demonstrating their virile virtues, the first of which was *strenuitas*, courage. It was at tournaments that, one after the other, they amassed booty, won glory, polished up a brilliant reputation and accumulated the symbolic capital from which Arnold, their descendant, would benefit. It was to tournaments that heirs waiting to inherit, and all the young men condemned to celibacy by family policies, went in order to let off steam, vent their aggression and nurture their hopes: the battles over, would not the most valiant of them receive a wife? Lambert kept this dream alive among the 'bachelors' who listened to him, offering them, as example, one of the lords of Ardres, Arnold II, great-grandfather of his patron. All day, he had shone before the powerful sire of Alost. The latter, already impressed by 'rumours of the honour and magnificence of his chivalry', welcomed him and his team to his tent at the end of the battle. They drank long into the night. In the morning, when they had slept off the wine, Arnold received one of his host's sisters as a gift. It is a splendid story, but it is clearly misleading. Detailed negotiations between the two houses had preceded the gift, and the count of Flanders, lord of the Alost and of the Ardres, would certainly have had his say. This is not to deny that various Guiniveres or Fenices, attentive spectators and connoisseurs of feats of arms, sus-ceptible, married or unmarried, weighed up from afar the strength of the men, or that the latter believed it possible to earn the favours of one or the hand of another by acquitting themselves well among the perils of these fierce confronta-tions, which were like fairs, fairs for the champions and fairs for the women. The ecclesiastical authorities condemned them as 'execrable' and Lambert repeated the word. This was because the knights damaged each other, and because they met their deaths in tournaments as often if not more often than in war. One of the distant ancestors of the counts of Guînes was believed to have lost his life in the Ile-de-France in one of these ferocious encounters. It was said that the peasants, his subjects, whom he oppressed, had been overjoyed. When he had set out, they had all hoped he would perish there. Tournaments were loathed by the people because at them, spending more than they gained from ransoms, the sires ruined themselves. They returned greedy, eager to put up taxes. Arnold of Guînes, who had spent eleven years travelling from tournament to tournament, followed by all the disruptive elements of the land of Guînes, lost not only what he had been given by his father but that part of the tax levied in preparation for the third crusade which he had received to equip himself.

At the time when Lambert was writing his book, to fight properly, provided with modern equipment, was becoming increasingly expensive and war was more prevalent than ever. The two principalities had developed on a frontier, between dry land and stagnant waters, between the Germanic and Romance dialects (like, probably, everybody else in the house in which he served, the priest of Ardres spoke both, but the masters and their officials affected to use primarily Romance, the language of the courts), and also a political frontier, the land of Guînes squeezed between two strong states, the county of Flanders and the county of Boulogne. In the years leading up to the battle of Bouvines, this fractured zone was put into a state of ferment. At Bouvines, in 1214, Count Arnold, the hero of Lambert's narrative, by then an old man, even older than Philip Augustus, would be present in the camp of the king of France. But between 1194 and 1203, loyal to the closest of alliances, cemented by family and friendship, further strengthened when the lordship of Ardres had been created within the county, he and his knights lined up under the banner of the count of Flanders, then in open conflict with the king. The latter, first in the name of his wife, then in that of his son, had seized Artois, Saint-Omer and the homage of the county of Guînes. His hold on them was firm since his friend Renald of Dammartin had, thanks to him, become count of Boulogne. But he was brought into conflict with the count of Flanders, and behind him the king of England. In 1194, when Richard Coeur de Lion returned from captivity, hostilities flared up again, and never ceased. During the summer of 1197, Philip Augustus advanced as far as Ypres, devastating the enemy territory. He was forced to withdraw, and it was Arnold of Guînes who conducted the siege of Saint-Omer, which was defended by one of his cousins, 'his great friend'. He built a tower of wood, higher than the walls of the town, from the top of which he pelted them with missiles shot by his ballistas. He worked wonders. The grateful count of Flanders made him a gift of a large sum in sterling pennies, 'digging into the jars full of gold and silver that had been sent him by the king of England to fight against the king of France'. Arnold used the money to pay off his debts.

But although war could be immensely profitable, usually it was just the opposite. What was the cost to Count Baldwin, the father, of the great round tower, roofed with lead and surrounded by stone walls, a miniature Louvre, which he built at Guînes in the face of danger, or of his other fortifications at Audruicq and Sangatte? He was ruined. In the end, by one of those reversals so frequent in the course of feudal battles, this old man, in 1203, had to surrender his person as a surety to the king of France, with those of two of his younger sons, both knights. Arnold himself, at the end of his resources, was obliged to kneel with hands joined before Philip Augustus and acknowledge himself his vassal. Lambert wrote his book in dangerous times, to the sound of clashing arms. That it was never finished may be connected with this sudden reverse. Anyone who wishes to get a true picture of what women's lives were like in this place and at this time must allow for the permanent proximity of war and of tournaments, its simulation; women were never far from dozens of violent men, practising their horsemanship, furbishing their breastplates, smelling of sweat, leather and the piss of the horses they looked after more carefully than they did them; one must imagine them in great danger, shut up in the fortress, anxious, obliged sometimes to handle defeat alone, to go out in search of money for a ransom, and blamed if, like the wife of Sulpitius II of Amboise, they failed to negotiate the release of a captive husband. Nor can the true power of women be properly appreciated if one forgets that the husband was away for most of the time, campaigning elsewhere, out of reach, and that though they might then live more freely, they nevertheless bore heavy responsibilities, and were, as people said, 'desolate', alone, without guidance, left to their natural weaknesses.

When he looked at the world around him, Lambert saw firstly households, relations of familiarity between the head of the house and his commensals, those people with whom he shared his meals and among whom he distributed all that his lordship brought in. This was his duty: he took with one hand and gave with the other. Not only his prestige but his real power depended on his largess. Misers were bad lords, who sometimes fell victim to their stinginess and died a bad death, like Arnold III of Ardres, whose throat was cut by his men, for whom he had failed to provide adequately. Lambert saw the population of the country as a whole as forming one vast household, organized on the model of the house of Ardres, where, among the boys of all ages whom the master prided himself on maintaining and took pains to make love him, he had lived 'from his infancy until he reached manhood'.

This house was old. It was of wood. It had been erected on the motte, a century earlier, for the great-grandfather of Lambert's patron. The carpenter who had built it was a skilled craftsman whose name, Louis, a king's name, was still remembered. This building, regarded as an architectural masterpiece on account of its complex internal fittings, and the pride of the household, was divided into two parts, one of which was set aside for women. This was a society which took care that the feminine and the masculine were strictly separated, assigning each to its place; the decision of the count of Guînes, around 1195, to divide the sick of each sex between two leper-houses resulted from this same concern. In Arnold's house, the main storey was divided into two. On one side were the quarters of the men, the open area of conviviality, the hall where the lord welcomed his guests, seated in majesty, eating and offering food to others, and where his companions and his servants lay down at night to sleep. On the other side were the women's quarters, enclosed, arranged round the 'great chamber', round the bed 'where the master and the lady slept together', the 'secret part', flanked by a cubbyhole for the maidservants, a dormitory for the children and a nursery for the babes-in-arms; and lastly, overhanging this sort of cocoon arranged for licit procreation and the careful rearing of the seigneurial couple's children, there was the place where, in the evening, the unmarried girls, daughters of the sire and of his knights and his priests, 'were locked up as was proper'. In principle, women left this area only to go to the chapel, or to the loggia where people met and talked, or to parade in all their splendid finery in the hall, on great occasions, with the permission of the lord.

In practice, the compartments were far from watertight. Most of the many women who lived in the house had difficulty escaping the attentions of lustful men. It is clear that the 'great chamber' was not the only place where people slept together and that the wife was not the only woman to give birth inside the house. Lambert never refers to the simple serving maids with whom the ordinary domestic servants amused themselves, but he mentions some of the women whom the masters of the two houses had favoured with their particular attentions. He had known several of them himself: Helwide and another 'maid of Ardres', who each gave a bastard son to sire Arnold III; Adela, daughter of Canon Raoul, whom Baldwin, Arnold's brother and successor, seduced before he went on crusade; Natalie, daughter of Canon Robert, by whom the same Baldwin had a son; and 'the very famous' Marguerite, mother of at least two sons, one by a brother of Count Baldwin, the other by a canon of Thérouanne. These are the only women Lambert names; in his youth, he had been friendly with their sons. It is enough to make it clear that in the castle of Ardres, as in that of Guînes, the master lived surrounded by concubines, like the dukes of Normandy two centuries before them. At his death, Count Baldwin left ten legitimate children, but, according to the chronicle of Ardres, twenty-three others who were illegitimate also wept at his funeral. Things had changed, however, in two ways. The bastards born of these relationships did not expect to succeed; when Arnold and Baldwin of Ardres died without legitimate heirs, none of the many boys they had fathered disputed the inheritance with the daughter of their sister. Second, if the Count Baldwin who kept a close eye on Lambert's work liked to hear it said that 'from the first stirrings of adolescence until his old age, the barely controllable turbulence of his loins filled him with an impatient need to copulate', he wanted it to be believed that neither he nor his ancestors had pursued young virgins, little girls, *juvenculae puellulae*, as long as they had a wife in their bed, and that they had permitted themselves these lapses only in their unstable youth or during their lonely years as a widower. In fact, in a well-ordered house, it was assumed that the wife was sufficient to quell the ardour of the master; this was one of her jobs. Obediently, the *curé* of Ardres endeavoured to convince his audience that this was how it had been.

The partition between men and women, between the public for the former and the private for the latter, went without saying. The whole social order was based on it. Lambert noted another partition, in his eyes both obvious and necessary. He knew that two sorts of dishes were prepared in the castle kitchens, the 'very refined' for the masters and the 'ordinary' for the servants. In the past, he had seen the maternal grandfather of his hero Arnold permanently surrounded in his house of Ardres by at least ten 'familiar' knights, a chaplain and several clerks, and he had seen him served by a domestic staff, 'of the most honourable', certainly, and maintained 'very generously and with a magnificent sufficiency', but nevertheless separated by a deep chasm from the men of war and the men of prayer; there were two classes within the household. There were two classes outside the seigneurial residence, too; the same line of demarcation passed between 'masters' and 'subjects', between nobles and non-nobles, between the free and the servile. It passed also through the women, separating those of the people from the wife, daughters, sisters, cousins and female bastards of the lord, of his knights and of the priests who surrounded him. Married and unmarried ladies were ranked with the canons, with the 'peers of the castle' (there were twelve at Ardres and twelve at Guînes, as there were round the count of Flanders and at the court of the king of France, and as there were knights of the Round Table and disciples of Christ) and with the 'vavassors' and other men of war. As a priest, Lambert was on the right side of the line. He was very close to the family of the master. He had married one of his daughters to the legitimate son of a bastard of the great-uncle of Arnold his lord. The blood of the 'great men of Ardres' ran in the veins of his grandson, who was called Baldwin after the count. He was not himself

a member of the family, which is why, in his history, he
pretends to repeat the words of someone better qualified
than he, the bastard son of another great-uncle of Arnold,
who preserved the memory of the exploits of the ancestors
and, a living book, recited them on demand before they were
written down. This does not prevent his evidence from being
of the very highest value. He had lived in close proximity to
the majority of the women whom he had brought back to
life. He had seen them as they were seen by the 'masters', the
'nobles' and the 'free men', his companions at table, and the
image of them that he presents is no different from theirs.

2

The Witness

This image was polished with loving care by the priest of Ardres, employing all the refinements of his culture. He bore a title, 'master', of which he was not a little proud. He had, in fact, received an excellent training in the 'liberal arts', to which his sophisticated style of writing, his taste for etymology and the quotations from Lucan, Horace and Statius which came naturally to his pen bear witness. In the prologue, he pays homage first to Priscian, that is to grammar and the art of writing good Latin, then to the classics, Ovid in particular, but also Virgil and the *Aeneid*, which he calls 'divine'. He even refers to Homer and Pindar. He may have acquired all this learning at Thérouanne, in the vicinity of the bishop, but it is more likely that it was at Saint-Omer, thanks to the links between the collegiate church and the master of the house in which he was brought up and the parish church in which he served. He had probably succeeded his father and he certainly preceded one of his two sons, who were, like him, priests; the fact that he was married seems to have shocked no one, even though it was over a century since the reforming prelates had embarked on their fierce battle to impose celibacy on all the servants of God. He had certainly worked in the library of the abbey of Saint-Bertin, and consulted the Flemish chronicles there. He saw himself as a historian, and took Eusebius, Bede and Sigebert of Gembloux as his models. He was the perfect representative of good ecclesiastical culture.

He was also very open to the other culture, profane, oral and poetic. His allusions to *Gormond et Isembart* and to 'Andrew of Paris' (whom I persist in identifying with Andrew the Chaplain) show him to have been aware of what was newest in the courtly literary output of his day. His work demonstrates that late twelfth-century phenomenon, the osmosis between the culture of the clergy and that of the knights, a fusion which was encouraged in this part of Europe both by the persistent vigour of Carolingian traditions in the great religious establishments and by the patronage of princes. Philip, count of Flanders, promoted Chrétien de Troyes, Baldwin of Hainault had all the Romance texts searched for references to his ancestor Charlemagne, and a similar appetite for knowledge and taste for literary works spread in more modest courts like that of the advocates of Béthune. The heads of many noble houses were keen to appear as well read as the great lords. They attracted into their houses masters who were capable of translating from Latin the authors who were debated in the schools. They had the poems that the *jongleurs* recited transcribed. They liked to read.

In 1160, or 1170, one of these enthusiasts and patrons was none other than the head of the household in which Lambert had spent his youth, the heir to the count of Guînes, who, while waiting to succeed, lived at Ardres in the house of his wife, that is, Baldwin, father of Arnold. Lambert extolled the intellectual qualities and culture of this man, who had brought him up, whom he both feared and flattered. He may have exaggerated, since he said what Baldwin wanted to hear. Baldwin prided himself on being *illiteratus*, whilst at the same time claiming to be able to recount *mirabilia*, 'marvels', and to know the 'letters' without ever having learned them; he had listened to the ecclesiastics who, during the offices, had read the Bible in his presence (Lambert specifies: the Books of Prophecy, the Historical Books and the Gospels). This was how, in the chapel, and by participating in the liturgy, the initiation of the knights into the sacred science began. They listened, but also remembered. Baldwin described himself as a *conservator* as well as an *auditor*. He could retain things. Through memory, sharpened by the demands of an oral culture, he became 'quasi-literate'.

He could therefore speak in his turn; he could engage in a dialogue with the clergy and expound before them the things that he knew about, the lore of fighting men. What did this consist of? I quote from the sixteenth-century translation: 'the amusing things that he had heard in the tales and stories of the poets'. Thus there was an exchange, and discussion. For Baldwin possessed to a high degree that virtue so precious in social circles which did not employ writing: *eloquentia*, loquacity. The fusion of the two cultures, chivalric and clerical, oral and literary, was achieved during the course of a debate, an *altercatio*, a war of words. This was an exercise in common use in the ecclesiastical schools. Here we see it transposed to the house of the lord of Ardres, where 'learned men', with whom the master liked to debate, were made welcome. He asked them to repay his generosity by writing books for him. In fact, 'Count Baldwin burned to embrace the knowledge of everything' (*amplectare*, to take it in his arms; in this womanizer, the thirst for knowledge went along with the appetite for sex). But he could not, obviously, learn 'the knowledge of everything' by heart. Extra memory was therefore preserved in books.

These were books which the lord might at any moment consult. Not directly, since he was unable to read and proud of it, but through the intermediary of 'men of letters' who read the text before him, translating it into the Romance language, also explaining it to him, commenting on it and guiding him from the first meaning of the words towards their 'spiritual interpretation'. Through these men, through Master Alfred or Master Geoffrey, through Simon of Boulogne, a local man who was one of the authors of the *Roman d'Alexandre*, Baldwin knew, 'learned' and understood, in addition to the Sunday Gospels and corresponding sermons, the Song of Songs, the 'book of St Antony' and works dealing with the nature of things and with the curiosities of the creation. It was, nevertheless, a layman whom the count made responsible for his library, a man who knew how to read, but only Romance, which proves that some of the books were written in the language of the courts. Reading and discussion took place in the hall, 'publicly'. The whole family, indeed the whole household, including Lambert in his youth, profited when Baldwin held forth within the house, equalling, said his panegyrist, both the finest experts in the Latin authors and the most celebrated *jongleurs* in the three genres of chivalric literature: the *chansons de geste*, the 'adventures of the nobles' and the 'fabliaux of the non-nobles'. In a similar fashion, the two cultures mingled in the person of the priest of Ardres. He had learned Latin in a cloister, but he was married and the father of a family. He knew what a family was and he knew what women were, and this makes his work infinitely precious.

'I ought', he says in the first lines, 'to have devoted myself entirely to my priestly duties, but, urged on by my patron, Arnold, the young lord of Ardres, I embarked on a difficult enterprise.' In fact, the command came from higher up, from Count Baldwin himself, the father. In 1194, he was preparing for the wedding of his eldest son. Lambert, accompanied by his own two sons, both priests, was about to set out for the chamber of the castle of Ardres, in order to bless the marriage bed. Baldwin ordered that the bells should first be rung as a sign of jubilation. Arnold had been excommunicated; carried away during one of his campaigns, he had destroyed a mill belonging to a widow. Matters had been arranged with the bishop and the archbishop, the sentence had been lifted, and the wedding could be celebrated with all the desired pomp, but Lambert was still unaware of this. He took the time to check the position before ringing the bells. The delay was slight, at most two hours, but Baldwin's anger was terrible. Abused in the middle of the town, in front of his church, the terrified *curé* of Ardres fell from his horse in a faint, then, repentant, set off at a gallop in pursuit of the count. Baldwin calmed down, but, said Lambert, 'never since, except when he had need of me for his affairs, did he behave to me in so friendly or cheerful a manner as before', and, he went on, 'to

recover his love and his favour, I undertook to buckle down
to this work'. Let us accept the anecdote for what it is, an
expression of allegiance to the old lord. At least it establishes
that the marriage of the heir was the occasion for the composition of the genealogical narrative.

It was a late marriage, long-awaited, and profitable.
Arnold was nearing thirty. Thirteen years after he had been
dubbed, a wife worthy of the renown of his house, whose
value would attest to the power of the principality, was still
being sought. Having just failed to get the heiress to the
county of Boulogne, they had fallen back on one of the
daughters of the count of Saint-Pol, had then found someone
better and had broken the marriage agreement. Now, a
woman was about to enter the chamber and the bed which
had been empty for the seventeen years since the death of his
mother, and she was bringing a fine lordship, which adjoined
the county, the castellany of Bourbourg. This success must
be celebrated. A new link was being forged in the chain of
lineage. To add lustre to the new husband and 'his glorious
father and the progeny of both', a carefully and elegantly
composed book would relate the great deeds of Arnold's
ancestors, maternal and paternal, and evoke their deaths, in
lasting form, in written, fixed, words, and would restore
them to earthly life in all their glory.

Lambert dealt with the two genealogies in succession,
beginning with that of the Guînes, respecting the hierarchies:
the counts were of higher rank, the masculine certainly
outclassed the feminine, and the paternal lineage took pre-
cedence over the maternal. He traced the history of the
counts up to the time when his patron, Arnold, abandoned
the ritual roving of new knights and gave up tournaments,
when, having returned to the fold after a long period of
restless wandering, and having soothed the resentments of
his father, the prodigal son 'behaved in everything according
to the wishes of his said father' and got ready to accept the
wife he had chosen for him. Passing to the other dynasty,
Lambert took up the history of the Ardres at its origins and
traced the dynasty up to Arnold's marriage. Eight or nine
years had passed since he had set to work. Having reached

this final point, he continued to write and described several memorable events which had taken place since the wedding. At the heart of the work, where the two lineages are joined together, he placed two portraits of men, that of Baldwin (sixteen chapters) and that of his son (seven chapters): he describes two stages of life and two types of male behaviour, one characterized by wisdom, the other by impetuosity.

Lambert had seen four or five of the lords of Ardres at close quarters. He prayed specially on certain days for those who were dead. He could question older men than himself within the house, trusting to their memory as to his own, and he showed little inclination for pursuing the oral enquiry beyond the domestic circle. In the case of the Guînes, he was less at ease. The origins of the family went back much further. He needed, therefore, to search in books. But most of his information certainly came to him from the Count Baldwin of whom, we know, he liked to speak and who was blessed with a long memory. The recollections that were recovered in this way form three superimposed strata. The most recent covers some forty years. As far back as about 1160, when Count Baldwin married the heiress of Ardres and went to live in her house, Lambert is clear and accurate. He records five precise dates, all of which concern the Ardres. Dates are rare in this work; the rules of this literary genre, the *historia*, forbade citing too many of them. Two are funerary: 1169, the death of Baldwin's father, and 1177, the death of his mother. The third, 1180, was the year when Arnold was dubbed. The last two dates concern the patrimony: around 1176, an old man with a white beard turned up in the region, claiming to be the lord Baldwin who had died in the East twenty-eight years earlier, momentarily striking fear into the house lest he should claim the inheritance; in 1198, the lord Arnold, thanks to the generosity of the count of Flanders, was able to pay off his debts. Further back in the past, the memory is less sure, though fairly firm as far as the last third of the eleventh century, time of Arnold I of Ardres and Baldwin I of Guînes. There are a few chronological milestones: the foundation of the collegiate church of Ardres in 1069 and of the monastery of Andres in 1084.

Further back still, all is obscure. There are names gleaned
from cartularies or from epitaphs, and one date, 928 (where
Lambert got it from, we do not know), year of the return to
the land of his fathers of the founder of the comital dynasty.
This is where Lambert's history begins.

The work is assigned three functions. The first is moral. It
would demonstrate to the descendants the virtues and the
faults of their forebears, teaching them that the young ought
to defer to the old and that every lord deserved the preroga-
tives he enjoyed only if he was a brave and generous knight
and faithful vassal. This lesson was entirely aimed at men,
and the models are all male. The second function is defensive.
Lambert was writing, through that of the two families, the
history of a country, of a nation, albeit a tiny one, that was
angustissime, threatened. This book was capable of protect-
ing it. In fact, an object of this type, a book made up of
leaves of parchment covered with signs that only the initiated
could read, and which they transposed into a series of words
spoken solemnly, still seemed at this period to be endowed
with an unquestionable tutelary power. Lambert's history
included a demonstration of this. When Baldwin of Guînes
founded the monastery necropolis, he had conveyed to it
some recently discovered bones that he kept in his castle
chapel. They were, it was said, the relics of St Rotrude, who
became the patroness and protectress of the abbey of Andres.
To make this invisible personage more real, the monks placed
near to the reliquary a book containing the story of her life.
It was read every year in the refectory, 'at dinner, on the day
of the solemn feast of the said virgin, to the audience of those
who were at table'. Everything the community owned
belonged firstly to God and then to Rotrude. So it was an
attack on her personally that was made, one day, by a lord
who was contesting the rights of the monks. In order to
destroy her power, he set out to burn both the relics and the
book. The relics were miraculously saved and, once peace
was restored, they were ostentatiously exposed before the
eyes of the people. The book, however, was burned. The
monks made haste to rewrite it. It was a shield against future
aggression. The manuscript of Lambert's history had a

similar role. It summoned up the ancestors who had held the patrimony legitimately and who were there, in the shadows, threatening anyone who tried to disinherit their heirs. Lastly, this memorial celebrated the nobility of the two families. For this, their founder had to be located in the distant past, and this is what Lambert tried to do. To go back to the beginning was inevitably to come up against a woman. In fact, we find one woman at the origins of the maternal branch, whose role is active, and another at the origins of the paternal branch, whose role is passive.

3

Mother Goddesses

I t was not particularly difficult for Lambert to present the genealogy of the lords of Ardres in its entirety. It was short, going back little more than a century. Arnold, the builder of the motte, was still alive; as a child, Lambert had mixed with his grandsons and with many old men who could still remember the ancestor clearly. But where had this Arnold come from? There was a rumour in circulation which was objectionable to the family. It said that Arnold's father, a certain Herred, surnamed Cangroc, which in Flemish meant that he wore his coat inside out, was a labourer, a peasant, and a miser to boot; to save his only tunic, he reversed it when he went out to plough. In short, he was a serf. This was not true, said Lambert. Herred was of very good blood. What is more, and above all, he was not the father of Arnold I but the husband of his mother. And Lambert deliberately made this woman, Adela, whose name he may have made up, the founder of the dynasty, and a very glorious one.

At some distance from the castle, at Selnesse, between the wood and the marsh, 'one finds today', he wrote, 'pagan remains, red tiles, shards from vases of the same colour, fragments of small vases of glass. It is a place where now, when one ploughs, one comes upon a track, or rather a road, hard and paved with stones, a highway leading from the marshes to the wood.' And in the wood itself, 'where it is thickest, there are large stones arranged in the form of an altar, joined together without cement, and on this altar are very old figures and images of saints.' Recent excavations in this spot have revealed, on the site of a Gallic station, the remains of a settlement of the Roman period, a *vicus* active in the second century. Lambert presents Arnold's mother as the heiress of the lords of this place, who had been very wealthy, as the scale of the ruins of their residence revealed. She was descended, he says, from these pagan lords who, in very ancient times, had converted to Christianity. Thus, through a woman, through this woman, the lineage had its roots far back in the depths of time. It could claim to be as noble, if not more so, than the noblest families in the country. Adela, what is more, was a fine woman, who lived her life freely and courageously. Abandoned by her family, she had lived alone, 'without a man to protect her or cheer her'. Count Eustace of Guînes, her cousin, pestered her 'more than was decent and honourable and more than was right'; he was determined at all costs to give her to one of his followers. She did not refuse, but dragged her feet. 'Wisely', she decided to hand over everything she possessed to the bishop of Thérouanne, her uncle, 'without regard for blood or lineage'. In other words, in contravention of every rule, she disinherited the men of her family, which, in Lambert's day, it was obviously impossible for women to do, even in order to redeem their sins by almsgiving. Next, like many landowners at the end of the twelfth century, a period when land was being feudalized, she received her property back from the prelate as a fief. It was then necessary for this fief to be armed, and defended against the designs of the count of Guînes. It needed a man's hand. Adela was given by her lord and uncle the bishop to a 'strong and valiant knight', Herred. A widow, she would have preferred to remain in this state. 'On the advice of the bishop and her other friends', she had to marry a warrior, also of good blood. From his seed, on the very first night of her second marriage, she conceived the Arnold with whom the story of the dynasty began. Everything that this son owned, the land on which the castle was built, everything owned after him by his descendants, right down to that other Arnold for whom Lambert wrote, the property, the honour, the power and the glory, all came from a woman, from the blood, the tenacity and the bravery of this woman.

To satisfy his formidable master Count Baldwin, and to trace the comital dynasty right back to its origins, Lambert had to go back to the dawn of time, leaping over some five hundred years. In this dizzy distant past, marvels abounded and the *curé* of Ardres accepted this without blenching. Less critical than his contemporary, William of Tyre, to whom 'the claim seemed false', he repeated in passing a legend, that of Lohengrin, which had emerged a century earlier in the memory of Godfrey de Bouillon and his holy mother Ida. Without batting an eyelid, he accepted that the first of the counts of Boulogne had 'come from the sky carried by a swan, not at all fantastic, but real and divine'. Nevertheless, in the case of the Guînes, he took care not to stray too far from what was reasonable. He searched for facts. In the library of Saint-Bertin, in 'tiny, very ancient pages', he found the name of a man, Galbert. At the beginning of the seventh century, this man bore the title of count in Ponthieu. He was a contemporary of St Bertin, and Lambert imagines him becoming a monk along with his only son, his brother and his sister. The land of Guînes, the only part of their patrimony that they did not give to the monastery, was thus 'widowed', deprived of a master to govern it, like a woman without a man. 'Without legitimate heir, little regarded', it was easy prey and it was usurped and taken over by the counts of Flanders. But two centuries later, in the time of one of these counts, Arnold the Great, God took pity on 'the lords and the people of Guînes, and provided them with an heir by just and hereditary possession'. This was a Norseman, a Viking, Siegfried. In 928 (we know that it was around this date that Rollo led bands of Normans to pillage Ponthieu, which suggests there may have been some historical basis for Lambert's story), this young man, 'noble of body and spirit, valiant, already very famous', arrived in the area. He had served the king of Denmark for many years and he had become, in Dacia, that distant land of marvellous exploits and sagas, second only to the king. Public report, but also, said Lambert, the reading of written genealogies, had informed Siegfried that he was of the blood of Galbert and that the land of Guînes belonged to him. With a few companions, he set out to make himself its master, and it was to this end that he built the keep of Guînes; he was a bold young adventurer, like Arnold I of Ardres, and like all founders of dynasties.

Nevertheless, a woman appears by his side, and it was from this woman that the new house derived most of its glory and its nobility. Starting from a name, Siegfried, the priest of Ardres concocted a love story of the type that people at court then enjoyed hearing declaimed. 'Flabbergasted' and seething with rage, Arnold the Great of Flanders prepared to expel the invader. He summoned his warriors to Saint-Bertin, and, to be sure they were in training, organized tournaments. Spirited and wise, Siegfried seized the initiative and made an appearance. He had friends in the count's entourage who mediated between them, and Arnold calmed down. He liked the look of the Dane, and welcomed him into his intimate circle. It is here, in the privacy of the household, that the woman makes her entrance. Elstrude, daughter of Arnold and sister of Baldwin, the new count, attracted Siegfried. He seduced her, coaxing her first by words, then caresses, finally taking her, without violence, in secrecy, and impregnating her. When the pregnancy became visible, he fled. To sleep with the sister of the lord without his consent was an act of treachery, deserving the severest of punishments. Siegfried escaped 'into his country', to Guînes. There, he soon died, 'from an excess of love for her he had been forced to leave'. Elstrude gave birth and her brother agreed to be godfather to her son. Captivated by this handsome godson, Baldwin made him a knight and installed him as count of Guînes on the land of his paternal ancestors. Why did Lambert opt for this fable and these clandestine embraces, for bastardy rather than what the documents make plain was a frequent occurrence in real life in the eleventh and twelfth centuries, that is the good vassal receiving in legitimate marriage one of the daughters of his lord in reward for his loyal service? Lambert repeated what people liked to say in the entourage of Count Baldwin. The count was by no means displeased to hear a historian confirm that the seed he carried derived from a reckless warrior, driven by Nordic *furor*, attractive to women, capable not only of recovering the inheritance usurped from his ancestors but also, if not of insinuating himself into the bed of the usurper, at least of taking and enjoying one of the women the latter kept under his thumb. He was a ravisher, consequently, but in the manner of the times. By the twelfth century, rape has given way to courtly love, in the Parisian fashion, and the hero of the romance, a new Tristan, died a slow death from the pains of love. But Baldwin also wanted it to be known that he was a direct descendant of the counts of Flanders and, through them, of the Carolingians. Lambert's history, consequently, as it says in the preamble, runs from one Arnold, the very famous Arnold the Great, to another Arnold, the lord of Ardres, soon to be count of Guînes. A woman, Elstrude, had transmitted the blood of the first Arnold to the second, who, bearing the same name, was called on to revive his outstanding merits.

Guînes and Ardres were not the only houses to place a woman at the source of their greatest prestige. The counts of Flanders, the counts of Anjou and the sires of Amboise also revered the memory of a female founding forebear. For the Flemish, it was Judith, daughter of Charles the Bald and great-granddaughter of Charlemagne. This woman was not seduced by Baldwin I, grandfather of Arnold the Great, himself a new man, the name of whose father was unknown until, during the course of the eleventh century, the scholars devoted to the comital lineage provided him with some ancestors; he carried her off by force, before he succeeded in getting her solemnly granted to him as his wife, in 862. Judith has pride of place at the centre of the oldest piece of writing conserving the ancestral memory of the Flemish princes, a sort of liturgical poem which the canons of Compiègne offered to Count Arnold the Great in the middle of the tenth century. She stands at the junction of two genealogies, that of the 'very noble emperors and kings of

the Franks' and that of the 'holy lineage of monseigneur
Arnold, most glorious count, and of his son Baldwin, whom
the Lord deigned to protect in this world'. Before her name –
Judith – the scribe has placed a cross, and another when he
repeated it. She is the only person in this long text whose
presence in the memory was sacralized by this device, the
only women we see honoured with a panegyric celebrating
this female forebear for her 'prudence' and for her dazzling
'beauty', and recalling that the first of the counts, Baldwin,
the 'most strong', was joined to her 'by matrimonial union',
that is, legally. Everything is arranged around the woman
through whom the stock became 'holy'.

Judith also holds pride of place at the centre of the two
genealogies written by a canon of Saint-Omer, Lambert, in
1120, when the new count of Flanders, Charles, surnamed
the Good, came to hold a solemn court in the collegiate
church. In the first of these genealogies, the historian is
careful to demonstrate the legitimacy of Judith's marriage.
The justification was necessary because the morality of good
conjugality that the Church had fought hard to get accepted
now prevailed. So Lambert of Saint-Omer established that
Judith, widowed by the death of a first husband, returned
home as she should to the house of her father, and that,
while it was true that Baldwin had abducted her, it had been
in collusion with her brother, which made the capture less
brutal; this woman had been half-granted by the men in her
family. Lambert recalls that Baldwin and Judith were at first
excommunicated in accordance with the canonical precepts
punishing the rape of widows, but that they were absolved
by Pope Nicholas I and that, at the request of the papal
legates, Charles the Bald finally gave his consent and allowed
his daughter to be joined 'according to the law of marriage'.

On the next folio of the *Liber Floridus*, the anthology in
which writings of all sorts, most of them historical, are
brought together, a second genealogy is transcribed. This one
takes the form of a poem; it was perhaps sung, chanted
during the ceremonies at which the count displayed himself
in all his power. In fact, the two last verses celebrate in him
'the son of the king', hailing him as new sovereigns had been

hailed since Charlemagne. This sequence of forty verses is
dominated by the same woman. Like a man, and like the
counts, Judith is named twice. Like them, she is the active
partner in the procreation of the successor. It is not said of
her, as it is of the other countesses, that she passively received
the seed of her spouse. It is said that she gave him the son
who would in his turn assume the honour. She was a donor,
and, in fact, she gave much more than this. Through her,
Charles the Good could trace his ancestry back to the
ancestors of the Carolingians and, through another woman,
much further back still, beyond the Merovingian dynasty, as
far as 'Priam, prince of the Trojans, stock of the noble
princes, the Franks and the Flemings'.

I have already remarked how the count of Anjou, Fulk
Réchin, reciting his own genealogy in 1096, mentioned only
men, with the exception of his own mother. At the origins of
his lineage, he put Enjeuger, and his memory was sound.
Modern scholarship has confirmed that this man was the
first of his stock to exercise, in the name of the king of the
Franks, the power to command and to punish in the county
of Anjou. He owed this 'honour' to his valour. Like Siegfried,
he incarnated victorious daring, the virile virtues. No one
saw Enjeuger as anything other than a self-made man,
succeeding by the strength of his arm, and no one imagined
that he owed anything to a mother or to a wife. Nevertheless,
half a century later, in a genealogy of the Angevins attached
to that of the sires of Amboise, there is a woman by
Enjeuger's side, and the story, later elaborated by John of
Marmoutier, shows the founding hero elevating himself at a
stroke by a fabulous feat accomplished on behalf of this
woman. She was his godmother, heiress of a count of
Gâtinais. She was accused of adultery and of having
smothered her husband. Like Adela of Selnesse, the men of
her blood abandoned her, refusing to fight on her behalf in a
judicial duel against the formidable champion of her accusers.
Trusting to God, Enjeuger, barely emerged from adolescence,
confronted and vanquished him. He did not receive, this
woman's body as the reward for his bravery, since a godson
could not marry his godmother. But, by royal decision, he

got everything she possessed, at the expense of her family, who were disinherited, as Adela's family had been. This property was the foundation on which the Angevin dynasty was based.

The lords of Amboise, too, claimed to owe their wealth and their fame to female forebears. At the beginning of the eleventh century, Lisois, a younger son and therefore obliged to make his own way, had served Fulk Nerra, count of Anjou, long and valiantly. Fulk was growing old. He wanted to provide his son with friends he could rely on. Before his son and all his assembled warriors, he declared: 'I wish to see by your counsel and by the counsel of my barons what I can give to Lisois for the great service that I have received from him. For I intend to retain him as a faithful follower for your benefit and for mine.' The provost of Loches, a friend of Lisois, advised Fulk to give him a young woman who held part of Amboise. There, the lineage would put down roots. The canon who wrote down the household memory in 1155 was a lover of ancient texts and curious about ancient times. He did his best to get back to the origins of the patrimony. He discovered a few facts, fragmentary and uncertain, jumped from one to the other, and through a mixture of scholarship and imagination, believed he had established that this estate had often, over the ages, been handed down by women. He had before his eyes not only books, including the life of St Martin, but a landscape, the site of a very old town. In Amboise, on the escarpment, he could see the ruins of a vast monument. It was called the 'old Rome'. The ghost of Caesar haunted the spot. He also saw three castles, side by side. He knew, he may even have seen, that three powerful men had lived there at the beginning of the twelfth century. To explain this threefold division, the historian delved deep into the very distant past, to the time of the Emperor Maximin and of the count of Tours, Avician, who had fortified the site. One woman, the daughter of Avician, had received Amboise as an inheritance, then another, her daughter Fausta, and lastly a third woman, Fausta's daughter, the 'good' and 'very wise', Lupa. This very Roman name is linked by the author to two toponyms:

Porta Lupa, a vestige of the ancient town where Fausta had established her residence, and *Villa Lupa*, Villeloin, a neighbouring village, where she had built a church and installed some monks, before retiring as a widow to a place close by this sanctuary, to lead a solitary life devoted to St Martin. After the death of her two sons, who were buried at Villeloin, the 'lady of Amboise' resisted the Goths. When a very old woman, she bequeathed all her lands to Clovis. This is where the first series of heiresses ends.

The Frankish kings held Amboise until the time of Charles the Bald, who shared the town between his faithful followers. To one of them, he gave two of the castles, and this portion eventually came into the hands of the counts of Anjou, again through two women, whom two of the counts, Enjeuger, then his son Fulk the Red, were able successively to marry. An orphan, Gersenda, inherited the other third. Her uncle, Sulpitius, administered the property in her name while waiting to marry her off. This was the man whom Fulk Nerra asked – or forced – to 'join his niece in marriage to Lisois along with the stone tower of Amboise that he had built with her money'. The new husband settled there. He was totally assimilated to the family of his wife, first by giving his son not his own name or that of his father, but that of Sulpitius, the man who had granted the third fortress, then by choosing to be buried at Villeloin, alongside Lupa the She-wolf; it is she who is seen, in this text full of fantasies, posted at the gates of darkness, venerable, venerated, a sort of mother goddess at the dawn of the family saga.

In this, she was like Adela, like Eltrude, like Judith and like the anonymous godmother of Enjeuger. Every dynasty started from a union of two people: from a man, a wandering warrior, come from an improbable elsewhere, who established himself through his prowess, and from a woman, sedentary, solidly established by her ancestors, her female ancestors above all, on a piece of land. The man took the woman and the land and set out to make both of them bear fruit. The female forebear was certainly less of a presence than the knightly hero in the memory of her descendants, but they were equally in her debt and they did not forget it.

4

The Couple

Lambert's *History of the Counts of Guînes* names many women, nearly a hundred of them. In the genealogical sequences, the names of the daughters of the head of the family are carefully listed after those of the sons, in order of birth, for each generation. All, or almost all, these women were married. It was for this that they had been brought into the world, to be scattered far and wide, and to make dead men – the Arnolds and the Baldwins, ancestors of the lineage – present everywhere in the person of their descendants. 'Bred in order to procreate offspring of good blood', was how Lambert bluntly put it with reference to the daughters of William of Saint-Omer. Women were obliged, consequently, to submit to the decisions of the men of the family, whose job it was to make profitable and judicious use of their procreative capabilities. 'Submission of the daughters who deserve the highest praise', Lambert said, a little further on, with regard to Agnes, one of the granddaughters of the same William. Because her maternal uncle had become prince of Tiberias, and because her cousins had discovered there, across the seas, a good family in which to place her, 'so that she would extend into the vast expanses of those distant lands the lineage of such famous ancestors', she had set out for the other end of the world. Scarcely had she arrived in the East when 'she died without having procreated for her father famous and wealthy descendants'; it was for her father, let us note, that it was her duty to bear sons, in return, or in exchange, for the life that he had given her. All the daughters of the lord were given, even those who were illegitimate.

A few, nevertheless, remained without husbands, watched over with great care. Some were kept at home, like one of the great-aunts of Arnold of Guînes, who remained a virgin to the end of her days. More often they were placed in a convent, one of those abbeys for women which proliferated during the twelfth century, established by lords so that their widow could retire there to lead a virtuous life after their death. In 1102, Count Manassé and his wife founded the monastery of Saint-Leonard; to direct it, they fetched from Lorraine a nun from within the family, of the lineage of the count's mother. When she was widowed, the countess went there to die. The nephew and successor of Manassé sent two of his eight daughters there and, one after the other, they became its abbesses. Some women waited for a husband there, as did Beatrice, the future wife of Arnold. Until her marriage, she 'learned good manners and was educated in the liberal arts' in the 'cloister of nuns' which stood next to the castle of Bourbourg, held by her father. One of her aunts had been buried there. Another bore the title of abbess, though it was not, in practice, she who gave the orders. Real power lay with a third aunt, the youngest, whom her parents had been unable to marry. Remaining a virgin, but not consecrated, she lived virtuously in her own home, on her share of the inheritance, off her own income. On the basis of her epitaph, Lambert lists her qualities: saintliness of life, wisdom, kindness and charity. He emphasizes the power of this woman. 'The whole convent, nuns as well as servants, were instituted, directed and maintained by her prudence.' One is reminded of Juette: a group of women without men under the iron rule of one woman, who also controlled the men who served and obeyed them. We see here the full extent of the power that a woman could wield in the society of the day. It was exercised in a sphere that was restricted, sacralized and shielded from male lust. It was where daughters repelled by marriage went to seek refuge. The chronicle of the monastery of Andres reveals that the eldest daughter of Arnold of Guînes refused the husband he had chosen for her; in 1218, she fled secretly from the paternal roof to shut herself away, safeguarding her virginity, in the abbey of Bourbourg, which her great-aunt directed and where her mother later chose to be buried. Was this a vocation? Or a call from God? Or was it the appeal of the model offered by the Church, which promised virgins three times as many merits as widows, and nine times as many as wives? It is perhaps more likely that this young woman knew only too well what men were like. She had watched them getting drunk on the evenings of festivals. She had seen her doddering grandfather chasing after little girls. Aware of the lot that this society reserved for married women, she did not want to be married; in this, she was like many others, like, for example, all those girls that Juette sheltered under her wing in the leperhouse of Huy.

Though Lambert mentions almost as many dead women as dead men, he does little more than record their names. This prolix text, written by a man for men, teems with the words and deeds of men. It is as if the women remained shut away in their own world, about which he says nothing because it was of no interest and because little was known about it. Of the thirteen women who succeeded each other at the head of the family, nine on the Guînes side and four on the side of the Ardres, Lambert tells us almost nothing. Christiana, the mother of his Arnold and wife of the Count Baldwin II he so feared, makes only three fleeting appearances in his story, in connection with her engagement, her pregnancies and her death. He says nothing of her virtues or her vices. Though he had served her, given her communion and ministered to her, the *curé* of Ardres tells us less about her than about the concubines. Indeed, in order to justify the lords for having enjoyed themselves with the latter, he emphasizes their qualities: they were not whores but noble creatures, they were still virgins and, lastly, they were all beautiful, with clear complexions and shapely bodies; who could resist such temptation? In the case of the wives, there

are no such eulogies, with one, hyperbolic, exception: that of
Beatrice, the heiress of Bourbourg. This still-young woman
would be a new Minerva, a new Helen, a new Juno, thanks
first and foremost to the value of her blood and her virginity,
then to her excellent morals and lastly to the charms of her
body; the description is banal. The only original feature, and
this is new at the end of the twelfth century, is that Beatrice
had been well educated at Bourbourg – she was 'literate'.

To a degree, this brevity is explicable; the wives of the first
three counts had been dead for over a century and the
household remembered only their names. In fact, it is by no
means certain that Lambert did not invent these names:
Mahaut, Rosella, Suzanna. Others of these women had
produced no children; it seems that their husband had never
slept with them. One, Peronella, was very young when her
husband, Arnold III of Ardres was murdered. Lambert
remembered her from the days when he had lived as an
adolescent boy in the seigneurial residence. He could still
picture the little child-bride very clearly; she was endowed in
his eyes with an eminent virtue, *simplicitas*, combined with
the fear of God. She divided her time between religious
observances and children's games, dancing with other young
girls, playing with 'dolls and other pastimes'. Often also, 'in
summer [the disturbing image surfaces from the back of his
memory], simple in soul and childlike in body, she undressed
down to her shift and plunged into the fishpond, not so much
to wash or to bathe as to cool herself down and take exercise,
swimming sometimes on her back, sometimes on her front,
sometimes under water, sometimes on the surface, showing
herself to be whiter than snow, or else, dry, in her bright
white shift, before the girls, but equally before the knights,
so demonstrating the sweetness of her manners, gracious,
amiable to her husband, to the men of war and to the
people.' The other childless woman, Beatrice, granddaughter
of Count Manassé, suffered from various illnesses. Her
health was failing, but even so, since she was the count's
only direct heir, her grandfather, on the advice of his wife
and in agreement with his family, had given her to a powerful
man capable of defending his rights. This husband had been

found in England, in the entourage of King William I. He did
not burden himself with the sickly wife, leaving her with her
family until he could make use of her, but he at once took
possession of the English estates she held through her grandmother. On Manassé's death, he went to Guînes to assume
the comital dignity, saw his wife there for the first time, and
almost immediately left, because 'he saw clearly that the
ailing Beatrice dreaded having to perform her conjugal
duties'. He left the field clear for other competitors. One of
them, Baldwin of Ardres, seemed to Beatrice's father to be
more useful than an English son-in-law. The unhappy wife
was therefore dispatched to England, accompanied by priests
and knights with instructions to negotiate a divorce. She was
brought back home, then handed over to a new husband.
But it was too late; she died before he could make her
pregnant.

The fate of the lordship had depended on this woman. By
taking her as his wife, a man of another blood had got hold
of the county. In some fifty years, this happened four times
in the two families whose history Lambert was telling. On
four occasions, the 'honour' died out and passed to a son-in-
law: through the Beatrice just mentioned, through Adeline
and her daughter Christiana, successively heiresses of Ardres,
and through another Beatrice, of Bourbourg. One sees how
closely the fate of patrimonies was linked to the quality of
women's bodies and to the fertility of wives. These four
hitches occurred because three wives, Emma of Guînes, her
daughter Rose, and Adeline of Ardres, bore only daughters.
This was an unhappy chance, not the result of a voluntary
restriction of births. The wives of this period knew very well
how to avoid being constantly pregnant. After providing her
husband with three children, the countess of Flanders decided
she had had enough and, says the chronicle, employed to this
end the 'artifices of women'. But these were rarely resorted
to. The majority of these wives were notably prolific. Christiana, the wife of Count Baldwin II, brought ten children
into the world who survived to adulthood. The last five died
in an eight-year period between 1169 and 1177. Her daughter-in-law, Beatrice, had already provided her husband

Arnold with six children when Lambert ceased to write. She went on to give him six more. At a time when, even in noble houses, infant mortality was high and accidents in childbirth were common, such an abundance, and the short intervals between births, speak volumes about the life these ladies led. Like Eleanor of Aquitaine, they went from one pregnancy to another, and their husband, who, we should not forget, was often absent, took full advantage of their procreative powers. Indeed, it is tempting to conclude that he abused them. Three of the nine wives who appear with any clarity in the *History of the Counts of Guînes and the Lords of Ardres* – that is, one in three – died in childbirth. There can be little doubt that physical love played a large part in the life of the married couple.

Of ties of affection, this narrative tells us very little. It records the place where five of the countesses were buried. Only one, the widow of Baldwin I, went to join her husband in the monastery necropolis. Two chose to be buried in an abbey for women: Emma at Saint-Leonard, which she had founded, and Beatrice II in the family convent of Bourbourg, alongside her aunts. Beatrice I chose to be buried near her mother in the Capelle-Sainte-Marie, Christiana near hers in the church at Ardres. It is as if, in death, the two sexes went their separate ways, as if the women kept to themselves, and the men likewise, as if, having shared the bed of their husband, the wives preferred to await the resurrection some distance away from him, among other wives, in a church where women prayed. Does this lack of enthusiasm for prolonging bodily proximity in death prove the lukewarmness of that mutual love which the husband felt it was incumbent on him to proclaim, that *concordia*, that harmony of hearts that Baldwin II wished for, when he blessed his eldest son and daughter-in-law in the marriage bed? What are we to make of the way this same Baldwin behaved? He was campaigning in England. His wife was about to give birth. Learning that she was unwell, he rushed to the scene, accompanied by two doctors. When she died, mad with grief, 'no longer knowing himself or anyone else, no longer distinguishing good from evil, the decent from the indecent', the doctors denied access to his chamber for two months to all but a few intimates able to look after him. Was he going to die of grief, like Siegfried, his distant ancestor, separated from his love? Obviously, Lambert was writing under the scrutiny of his patron, and sure of pleasing him by describing these demonstrations of violent conjugal love. What right have we, however, to dismiss this mourning as affected? Why should we refuse to believe that this husband was deeply hurt? The fact that all marriages were arranged by the families does not preclude at least some of them from being successful, or the couple from taking pleasure in their reciprocal love, or a certain tenderness from developing between them. We have to accept that the historian of these distant periods has no way of probing the secrets of hearts.

One thing, at least, emerges clearly from this family history. Although marriage agreements that committed very young girls were easily broken, the tie held after marriage and the union of bodies. None of the wives who appear in this book was repudiated. Admittedly, this practice was tending to disappear during the twelfth century. Matthew, son of Count Thierry of Flanders, sent back the woman his father had provided for him when he failed to have any sons by her. 'This girl had worn the habit of a nun since infancy, but she was the sole heiress to the county of Boulogne. So she was taken out of the cloister with the agreement of the pope [this authorization was necessary because she was a consecrated virgin, therefore already married, the wife of Christ]. She was joined to Matthew by marriage to give legitimate heirs to the paternal heritage . . . but after having fathered two daughters, her husband returned her to the cloister' and took another wife. His elder brother, Count Philip, however, behaved quite differently. His wife was sterile, but he made himself keep her as long as she lived.

Were these women, in the minds of the men who remembered their female ancestors at the end of the twelfth century, or in the minds of Lambert and the lords who commissioned his work, or in the minds of those for whom this book was intended, able to exercise power within the couple? And if so, what sort of power? The portraits of two women, Emma, wife of Count Manassé, and Gertrude, wife of Arnold II of Ardres, are clear enough to allow me at least to pose this question. As was usually the case, these two women were of better birth than the two men who had won them in their adventurous youth, by demonstrating their valour and in return for their assiduity in the service of the matchmaker. Emma came from a great Norman house, that of Tancarville, Gertrude from a great Flemish house, that of Alost. Gertrude had brothers, so she brought no lands, but her dowry in movable goods and in male and female servants was considerable. Emma had been given away by the king of England, along with fine lands in Kent. As a result, their husbands were disposed to treat them well. They did not, admittedly, owe them all their wealth. They did not, like Arnold I of Ardres, who owed his fortune to his second wife, go so far as to 'show them veneration in all things and everywhere, or revere them and serve them, not only as their wife, but as their lady'. The high quality of their blood and the power of their relations nevertheless gave Emma and Gertrude a certain influence over their husbands and over the men of the houses they had entered.

We are given a glimpse of Emma in the comital residence in a charter of the abbey of Andres dated 1117. One of the peers of the castle of Guînes is present; he acknowledges that he holds as a fief from the count a property the monks had just acquired from him. The count, before the assembled witnesses, solemnly approves the donation. His wife is by his side; they are both, says the charter, 'seated on their bed'. This, then, is how the spouses presented themselves in public, sitting on the same seat, the *domina* on the same level as the *dominus*, and seeming to share in the authority he exercises. This image suggests another, one that was beginning to be carved on the porches of the cathedrals of the Ile-de-France at the end of the twelfth century, that of Christ crowning his mother, associating her in his power, the two of them also seated side by side. But the count and the countess are sitting on their bed, which enhances the symbolic value, because the bed, throne of conjugality, was where spouses slept together and where wives gave birth, and because all the power permitted to the wife derived from her capacity to bear children. The same image of the bed also flows from the pen of Lambert. For him, Manassé and Emma formed a community of equals. They were associated, *consortes*, materially and spiritually, sharing 'the same bed and the same devotion': flesh and spirit. The *curé* of Ardres added that it was proper for the wife to 'kindle' in the heart of the husband 'the fire of divine love'. It was implicit that she ought also, this time in bed, to fuel that other fire, carnal love, in which healthy children were forged.

The association was a close one, a union of body and soul, the woman assuming the title of her husband – 'countess', 'chatelaine', 'lady' – and consequently sharing in his glory, necessarily present beside him in demonstrations of power; this is what it was conventional to show, and what society revealed, of the condition of women. But what was the reality beneath these appearances? We catch a glimpse in a little moral tale. At that time, Lambert recalls, a particular tax weighed on a section of the subject people, those descended from ancient immigrants; every year, on a fixed date, they had to take a penny, a tiny piece of silver, to the house of the master, and four pennies for a wedding or a funeral. This was the payment commonly demanded of personal dependants, of 'body' men and women (*homines de corpore*), as they were called, a sign of their servitude, of that 'servile stain' which meant that they were looked down on by their neighbours, who might be poorer than they but who were proud of their freedom. It happened that a man of status, a 'vavassor', married a girl everyone assumed to be free. On the night of the wedding, as the bride approached the marriage bed, 'hardly had she touched the wooden frame of the bed' when she saw officials of the lord enter the chamber. They had come to claim the four pennies. She blushed, 'both from fear and from modesty'. She protested, and was given the right to plead her case in a fortnight; we observe here the right women had retained to appear in court, not alone, admittedly, but 'accompanied by her parents and friends', and defending her cause herself, 'aloud'.

The case was dismissed. Her last resort was the lady of
Guînes. She went to speak privately to Emma, explaining the
danger women faced, threatened at any moment with being
covered with shame. The countess was persuaded and turned
to her husband. A little later, when night had fallen, in the
privacy of the bedchamber, 'she took him in her arms'.
'Cajoled', the count, in answer to the prayers of his wife and
of the misjudged woman, decided to abolish the infamous
tax. The memory of this female victory was preserved. A
lady had intervened in public affairs and she had influenced
their course. But how? In private, using her personal charms,
by embraces and affection, in sum, by exploiting her sex
appeal.

Lambert's memories of Gertrude were unhappy. She had
ruled over the household of Ardres when, as a boy, he had
been educated there. He had perhaps been a victim of the
'severity' of which he accuses her. He was certainly not
alone. He would not have judged her so harshly, describing
in his book how the people watched dry-eyed as she was
buried, and uttered the ritual lamentations 'hardly opening
their lips', nor would he have portrayed her as so arrogant,
'boasting of her nobility, seeking to elevate herself even
further by her haughty words', or so grasping, 'remaining
famous throughout the country for her avarice', had he not
been confident of pleasing his protectors. To demonstrate
Gertrude's greed, he told a story current in the household.
She had been made responsible for administering the family
property. Shrewdly, so as to take better advantage of the
pastures, she gave orders for all the beasts in the lordship to
be collected into one single herd. The officials who were
dispatched to arrange this regrouping arrived at the hovel of
a poor woman where there were seven children crying from
hunger. Their mother gave a hollow laugh; she had neither
cattle nor sheep; jokingly, she offered them one of her
children if the lady would like to 'put it to pasture'. Gertrude,
when she heard of this, accepted. She chose a little girl, and
'adopted her in the place of the lamb'; when she reached
marriageable age, she 'put her to a man', like a good farmer
anxious to increase the domestic livestock. In fact, when she

had received the child, she had made haste to impose on her the 'mark of servitude', after which all the offspring of this female serf would belong to her. At this point, Lambert remembered another young girl. She was one of the free women whom Gertrude had brought with her from Flanders on the day of her wedding, a young maiden, and very attractive. Many men had enjoyed and then rejected her. She had had enough, and asked a last lover, a manservant, to take her as his wife. The man refused, saying she was unworthy of him. She then went and knelt before the lady, making herself servile by the ritual gestures, placing her hands in hers, confident that the lady would help her once she became her chattel. She was not mistaken. She was quickly mated like a ewe, Gertrude forcing the valet to sleep with her, and so become himself a serf. Just as it was the job of the master to disperse his daughters and the daughters of his vassals beyond the house by marrying them off, so it was incumbent on his wife to order sexuality among the domestic servants, and to increase their number by collecting little maidservants from the peasant cottages, then providing them with a husband so that they would give birth to new dependants. This was a female power, within the household, a power that was autonomous, absolute and legitimate. Lambert criticized Gertrude's 'harshness' because she reduced to servile status the men she gave to her maidservants, and all the children born of them, and because, at the time that he was writing, serfdom was beginning to appear as the remains of an ancient barbarity. But he did not challenge the lady's power.

With regard to this power, we need to distinguish between the *res publica* and the *res familiaris*, between the inside of the house and the outside, the public and the private. In accordance with the model already being offered by prelates in the ninth century, when they described the perfect organization of the Carolingian palace, the lady was responsible for the 'economy'; her role was to maintain good order inside the house. Male and female servants were subject to her, but so were her own daughters and the daughters and sisters of her husband's vassals, whom she educated and whom she persuaded, more or less crudely, to accept the husband who was chosen for them. Perhaps we should allow for the rituals of courtly love and add the young knights whose apprenticeship had been supervised by her husband, and who projected on to her person not only their desire but the distant memory of maternal affection. In any case, the authority of the lady over female members of the domestic society was equal to that of those formidable women who, away from the world, governed communities of nuns. In the ultimate privacy, finally, that 'of the bed and its devotions', we may believe that she was the 'associate' of the head of the household. But, in contrast, as regards what happened outside, and public power, it would be dangerous to trust the public ceremonial. In practice, custom stubbornly refused to allow the lady to share with her husband the right to command and to punish. This was because she was a woman, and because it seemed improper and contrary to divine intentions for a female arm to brandish a sword; for power was symbolized by the sword, the sword that was solemnly handed over to the son of the master when he reached the age to direct a lordship, the sword that was placed unsheathed before the master when he sat in justice, and the sword that, in northern France at the end of the twelfth century, was beginning to be blessed and placed on the altar before the act of dubbing; it was the concrete image of the power that God delegated to those he charged with making peace and justice reign in this world by force.

Women were forbidden to shed blood. Joan of Arc was condemned also for this, for having acted like a man, for having, in the words of her judges, shown herself to be 'bloodthirsty'. When a woman inherited the power of command from her father, it fell to a man, the husband to whom she had been given, to wield the sword in her name, or rather in the name of the sons she had brought, or would bring, into the world, until the day they were capable of taking the sword into their own hands. It might be important for the heiress to stand beside this man at the moment when he exercised his right, so as to demonstrate the source of this right. But it was he who exercised it, not she. No doubt also, as what we know of the power of Emma suggests, the lady was regarded within the lordship as the official protectress of the female population. But she participated in public power only indirectly when, by exploiting her charms, she exercised a mellowing influence on her husband, persuading him to act less harshly. In the manual he composed for the use of confessors, Thomas of Chobham recommended imposing as a penance on married women that they should intervene ceaselessly with their husbands. No one, he said, was better able to soften the heart of a man than his spouse. Where and how? In bed, 'by embraces and caresses'. One of the virtues of ladies was clemency, and one of the functions of ladies was to introduce a little leniency into the exercise of power. This is what Our Lady did with regard to her son.

These seem to be the limits of the power of the wife, and they are strict. We may nevertheless assume that the sphere within which her power was exercised was frequently enlarged by the absences of the husband. As long as he had the strength, the knight was often away in search of adventure. The lady then enjoyed a freer hand. As long as he was alive, she did not go so far as herself to lead the warriors, except to organize the defence of the castle if it was besieged. But at the very least she was obliged to manage daily business, settle disputes and guarantee contracts. Because Count Thierry of Flanders was far away on the second crusade, it was Sybil, his wife, who received the homage of the new sire of Ardres. The latter's predecessor, Baldwin, had accompanied the count, and news of his death during the course of the expedition had just been received. Before it became known and before one of his brothers-in-law was designated to succeed him, did not his mother, the 'rude', 'harsh' and 'arrogant' Gertrude, briefly take the lordship into her own hands?

5

Widows

Gertrude was a widow, as Emma had been. These two, with Peronella, were the only ladies in the two families who survived their lord. But widows abounded in knightly society. Many women, admittedly, died young from complications in childbirth, but mortality was no less among men of war. They were decimated – by immoderate behaviour, and all sorts of excesses during a violent life, by the wounds received in the turmoil of tournaments and of battle, by the fevers caught campaigning in the East, sometimes by the blows of an assassin. Let us take as example Henry, castellan of Bourbourg, whose father and brother had been murdered by the side of the count of Flanders. Henry had seven sons. Two of them, provided with positions in the Church, died peacefully in old age, but of the five who were knights, not one succeeded him: one, blinded in a tournament, could not take over the lordship, the others died in various accidents before their father. And if many men died first, it was also because, having lost a first wife, they, like Louis VII of France, chose a second wife of tender years, then, overestimating their powers, overdid their amorous activities. *Uxorius*, too fond of sex, though warned by his doctors, Raoul of Vermandois succumbed in the arms of his wife Loretta. She was not without experience. When still a young woman, she had passed from the bed of the count of Louvain to that of the count of Limbourg and then to that of Yvain of Alost. The old Count Henry of Namur was next. She was clearly fertile and he thought she would be able to bear him a son. Disappointed, he grew tired of her and repudiated her; he then married a little girl, 'had her for four years without ever communicating (*communicare*) with her in bed', returned her to her father, then took her back and did his best, before dying, leaving a very young widow. It was in circumstances such as these that so many ladies of this period ended their days in freedom.

In practice, if they were still attractive and their sons still minors, they did not enjoy their independence for long; their own family and that of their deceased husband agreed to remarry them and did so without difficulty. Suitors fought over them in the often successful hope of seeing any children already born die before reaching adulthood, or of ousting them, in collusion with their mother, in favour of the children they would bear by her. At the least, the widows who were too faded to be desirable, or whose eldest son was old enough to succeed his father, remained free. They had to leave the house, and surrender their domain, the conjugal bed, to the new lord. They withdrew, but where to? The Church wanted women to retire into a monastery, like Emma at Saint-Leonard. It classed women, like men, into three ranked categories. But whereas, in the case of men, the tripartite division referred to the function performed in public life, whether it be to pray, to fight or to work to feed the others, in the case of women, the reference was to the degree of sexual purity: virginity, widowhood or marriage. 'Married life is good', said Lambert, 'but the continence of widows is better.' Widows were expected to renounce love. So that they would be less tempted to indulge in it, they were urged to shut themselves away in a cloister. In fact, many of them preferred to remain in the world, to exercise their power fully and, freed from the conjugal yoke, to enjoy themselves.

This was the choice of Ida II of Boulogne when she was widowed for the second time. Lambert took a jaundiced view of her. His hero, Arnold, had come close to marrying her

and the family took his failure badly. Lambert therefore
shows us a woman abandoning herself 'to the pleasures of
the body and the delights of the world'. Desired and desirable, less perhaps for her physical attractions than for the
prosperous principality of which she was the heiress, she
enjoyed seeing unmarried men revolve around her. She
played the game of love; she was, said Lambert, 'venereal'.
For more than five years, the young Arnold had been
strutting his stuff at tournaments in search of a good catch.
He found Ida to his taste. Fickle, as women were, she set out
to seduce him. Shrewd, like all men, Arnold played along
with her. He 'won the favour of the countess by making his
eyes burn with love, real or simulated.' What interested him,
according to Lambert's history, was Boulogne, 'the land and
the comital dignity'. Ida and Arnold exchanged messages,
discreetly, in the courtly manner, until something better
turned up. But a rival, Renald of Dammartin, was stalking
the same prey. Ida flirted with both, refusing neither one nor
the other; she inclined towards Renald, but she knew that
her uncle, Count Philip of Flanders, on whom her remarriage
depended, would not countenance a Frenchman from France.
So she declared herself 'once again touched by the flame of
the love of the said lord Arnold of Guînes'. No longer
content with words and messages, they met here and there,
on the borders of the two lordships, 'in chambers and secret
places'. An accident, the death at Ardres of one of her
servants, gave the countess a pretext to go openly to join her
lover in his own home. Arnold received her solemnly and,
once the servant had been buried, invited her to dine with
him, as if as a prelude to marriage. They talked at length.
The lady withdrew. Arnold 'would have detained her if she
had not promised to return very quickly'. Renald was
waiting. He abducted the more than half willing Ida, carried
her off to Lorraine and took possession of her. Perversely,
pretending to have been taken by force, Ida let the heir of
Guînes know that she would marry him if he came to her
rescue. Arnold set out with a strong escort. Renald had him
excommunicated, seized and incarcerated at Verdun.

Ida, it appears, was still attractive, or, at least, very

sprightly. Widows who had quietened down but who did not enter religion settled tranquilly on the dower. This was the portion of his goods and rights that the husband granted his wife at the time of the marriage treaty. If the future wife was worth it, the bids were raised, and this portion was considerable. Arnold of Ghent, future count of Guînes, gave everything he then possessed to get the daughter of the castellan of Saint-Omer, who was of Carolingian blood; his grandson, Arnold, did the same, offering the lordship of Ardres in order to marry the heiress of the castle of Bourbourg. While her husband was alive, admittedly, the lady had only a virtual right over this property. But once a widow, and if she remained one, refusing a second marriage, she took possession of the estate and, from then on, managed it freely, like a man. Let us take as example Mahaut, dowager countess of Flanders, who had settled at Lille, in her own home. She wanted to impose a tax on the inhabitants of the land of Bourbourg. She personally mounted a military expedition. Arnold of Guînes, her vassal, who held Bourbourg in the name of his wife, advanced in arms with the knights of the castle in order to protect his people. He did not have to fight and was relieved, 'for he had never been rebellious or disobedient to his lady, but had always taken trouble and persevered in the fidelity and loyalty that he owed her'. Mahaut did an about-turn, and he escorted her. She had acted in full possession of a male power.

Once their husband was dead, these women of mature years no longer stayed in the bedchamber, on the bed, but held court in the hall, and, at the end of the twelfth century, people grew accustomed to the sight of vassals kneeling before them, hands joined, or of litigants hearing their sentences. In fact, as public institutions achieved greater sophistication, the power of the state gradually became, at least in the great principalities, an abstract principle. That it should pass into female hands no longer appeared so scandalous. The time of female regents was approaching. And these widows proved all the more powerful in that they could rely on their sons, on the deep and warm affection of those sons who had been wrenched from them in early childhood, in particular the younger sons, whom they often preferred to their first-born. They then enjoyed to the full the power that was allowed to women. A few months after her death, the author of the *Deeds of the Lords of Amboise* wrote a deferential eulogy of Isabella, the widow of sire Hugh. He called her a *virago*, a strong woman, like Emma and like Gertrude. He called her 'favoured among all women', and the four Latin words that he chose to define what made her so remarkable express what qualities were celebrated in women in the twelfth century. They are *genere* (firstly stock, the quality of the blood), *forma* (after all, beauty of body mattered in a woman), *viro* (completed by the husband she had been given, since it was incumbent on the man to bring out women's qualities) and *liberis* (last and not least, favoured in the value of the children she brought into the world). The panegyrist added one quality, 'audacity', which he soon qualified as 'virile'. It was indeed this virtue that distinguished Isabella. The value of this female forebear lay in the fact that she had behaved like a man, suppressing the feminine in her. As a man, 'in a virile manner', she had set out to recover the land of her ancestors, alone, accompanied by her second son, who bore the sword on her behalf. 'In a virile manner', after twenty-five years of marriage, when, in 1128, her husband left her to follow the count of Anjou, his lord, and died in the Holy Land, she seized all the power that was available to her.

She was now fighting against her eldest son, Sulpitius. Before he had set out, in the hall before his assembled men, Hugh of Amboise had indicated this son as his sole heir. Sulpitius therefore wanted to keep everything that had belonged to his father. He did not relinquish the dower, and Isabella attacked him. It is striking how the tone of the story changes at this point, no longer admiring, but critical. The author of the *Deeds* was a man. Like all men, he was shocked to see a woman cling so fiercely to power. Isabella was 'virile', and she was admired, but she was a woman. She ought to remain in her station. Consumed by greed, by a fierce desire to enjoy the exercise of power, Isabella, in his eyes, in everyone's eyes, succumbed to what still remained of the feminine in her body, that is to say perversity. 'Avaricious', 'burning with fury', she caused disorder and broke the peace.

Peace was restored. The people of Amboise urged the son to live once again with his mother. Advent, time of repentance and forgiveness, was drawing near. They made it up and the dowager recovered her rights. She got part of Amboise, where she settled down in her own house, near to the church of St Thomas. Fifteen years later, she reappears in the narrative, this time in the role of a valuable mother. This time it was Sulpitius who got carried away; he had treacherously rebelled against one of his lords, and overreached himself. Isabella, standing in for the absent father, talked to him in the manner of all good heads of households exhorting their turbulent sons to calm down. These are the words put into her mouth by the learned canon who wrote the history: 'Why did you rush into this war without consulting me? Because I am infirm, do you think I am in my dotage? Rest assured, in my old body, the *animus*, the moral strength is still alive. You could not find better advice. What can compare with the *affectus* of a mother?' Her advice, then, was motivated by affection, by that intimate tie which bound, far more closely than the wife to the husband, the former infant to the woman who had carried him in her womb and suckled him.

The nature of women made them unsuitable to the exercise of public power. Some, nevertheless, managed to snatch a few crumbs, but discreetly, and by exploiting their feminine resources. When they were young, they played on the desire that the sight and the touch of their body aroused in the bodies of men, that of their husband and those of the knights of the court. In old age, they relied on the tender regard of their sons.

Women also enjoyed a more obscure power. For the leather- and metal-clad warriors of that age, who lived among other men, the women they encountered were strange beings. They imagined them to be linked by tangible ties to invisible powers, capable of attracting evil – for which they feared them – but also good – for which they venerated them. In fact, they credited women with a secret and very precious power: that to intercede on their behalf with the Father and judge. It is noticeable that the written texts from the provinces of Christendom which I have studied mention sorceresses, but not many of them. On the other hand, they reveal that female figures bulked large in the sphere of devotion, and this well before the end of the twelfth century, before the time, that is, of the emergence and rapid spread of new and specifically feminine forms of spirituality. Among these figures was the Mother of God. From the beginning of the eleventh century, the majority of new places of prayer were consecrated to her, including the oratory of the castle of Guînes and the monastery for men, the Capelle-Sainte-Marie, founded in 1091 by Ida of Boulogne (not the passionate and fickle widow discussed above, but her great-great-grandmother, the mother of Godfrey de Bouillon). In this abbey, Ida placed a reliquary covered with gold and precious stones containing eleven hairs of the Virgin, which were said to have been acquired from a king of Spain. And among the relics with which Arnold I enriched the church of Ardres were a 'minute portion' of this same hair and of the clothes of Mary, in a little cross. There were also women saints. When, in the 1080s, a packet of bones was discovered and taken to Count Baldwin I of Guînes, they were recognized as the relics not of a holy man but of a holy woman, Rotrude, who had become the protectress of the surrounding countryside. At Saint-Leonard, a convent for women, a book written before 1193 contains three lives of saints, that of the patron, Leonard, and those of two women, Mary Magdalen and Catherine. In honour of the latter, the wife of Count Baldwin II got him to build a chapel, and also to procure and deposit there a few drops of the oil that had emanated from the body of this virgin and martyr.

In the twelfth century, the Christian West created few male saints and even fewer female ones. On the borders of the land of Guînes, however, the ecclesiastical authorities had yielded to the pressure of the faithful and recently canonised two local women, Ida of Boulogne and Godeliva of Ghistelles. Ida was favoured because, an excellent mother, she had given birth to and fed with her milk the hero who had liberated the Holy Sepulchre, because, an excellent widow, 'her mortal husband dead, [she] seemed, without taking the veil, to be joined to the immortal husband by a life of chastity and celibacy', and, lastly, because she was generous and had provided for the monks just as she had provided for her sons, and she had striven to maintain on the path of virtue the group of young girls in her care. As for Godeliva, people went to the scene of her sufferings to beg for her approval and collect white stones which healed fevers because, a martyr to marriage, she had sacrificed her modesty to a wicked husband and patiently supported his humiliations, and because she had died strangled on his orders by his servants. The sainthood of these two women, whose manners and character, accentuated by the 'legends', symbolized two aspects of the condition of wives, one happy, the other pitiable, was officially recognized. But in private, within the family, people venerated other dead women.

I have noted three. The first is the Englishwoman whom the viscount of Marck, great-grandfather of Arnold of Guînes, had married, and whose remains, buried at the foot of the church tower, worked miracles. Portraits of the other two are sketched, probably on the basis of their epitaphs, in the very rich eulogy of the counts of Flanders completed at Saint-Bertin in 1163, to which a seventeenth-century printer gave the title *Flandria Generosa*. In this work, if the men are celebrated for their valour and, as they grew older, for their prudence and their wisdom, women were remarkable for their piety, in particular those elderly women who had 'voluntarily submitted to the stains of the flesh and been cleansed of their sins by repentance', subjecting themselves to the strict discipline of the 'order of widows' to which the death of their husbands had consigned them. The first, Adela, was the daughter of France given by King Robert to Count Baldwin V. 'Deprived of her husband but not of wealth, she nevertheless did not live in luxury in the midst of these riches. For her, they were dead. Adela spent her days and nights in prayer.' She even went to Rome so that the pope could solemnly introduce her into her *ordo*, bless her and invest her with the habit of widows. 'During the journey, she remained enclosed as if in a bedchamber, cloistered, a recluse, on a litter born by two horses, to protect herself from the wind and the rain but above all so as not to be distracted from holy meditation . . . She returned to die in the peace of Christ' at the monastery of Messines, which she had founded.

The third of these women to be venerated was Richilde, wife of Baldwin VI, who was remembered throughout the region, but ambivalently. Telling her story gave the monk of Saint-Bertin an opportunity to express what he thought about women. He held them in low esteem. He began by showing Richilde as an example of this intrinsic malignancy. She was, he said, throughout her life, a provoker of discord; she was a bad mother, who allowed the children of her first marriage to be dispossessed; she persisted in incest, treacherously forgetting the commitment made before her uncle the pope, and fornicating though this was forbidden; she was a usurper of power, tyrannizing the people in the name of her younger son, grasping, burdening Flanders with taxes, cruel, implacable and dissimulating; she bought King Philip and, at least half sorceress, she scattered enchanted powders and evil spells over her enemies. But this venom, this wickedness, all this cumulative wrongdoing, was wholly redeemed by the 'marvellous penance' the countess imposed on herself in her declining years. Like Mary Magdalen, she now never ceased to pray. Like Juette, she now devoted herself every day 'to the service of the poor and the lepers'. The biographer observed how, in his day, the women who were called beguines mortified themselves, and he attributed to Richilde, who had been dead for half a century, these new and extreme forms of female devotion. 'All covered in the puss of the lepers, she bathed them, then used the same bath water herself; sick like them, she hoped thus to become once again, internally, the daughter of the King.' She chastised her sinful flesh, she crucified herself, she destroyed herself. Eventually, she thus 'returned her body to the earth and her soul to the mercy of Jesus Christ'. So Richilde was at last purified of the violence, the greed, the deceitfulness and the lechery that the monk of Saint-Bertin described as *muliebres* because, according to him, they naturally infected the body of women. 'Her soul deserving to assume immortal perfection and to enjoy the delights of Paradise', she had taken her place, a helper, a mediator, beside Lupa, Ida and Denise, among those great tutelary figures who, deep down in the memory, watched over the destiny of lineages.

In the twelfth century, priests and warriors expected a woman, to be a docile daughter, a lenient wife and a prolific mother, and then, in her old age, by the fervour of her piety and the rigour of her renunciations, to bring a whiff of sainthood into the house which had received her. This was the ultimate gift she made to the man who had deflowered her as a young girl, who had mellowed in her arms, whose piety had been rekindled by her own and who had many times deposited in her womb the seed of the sons who would later, when she was a widow, support her, and whom she would assist by her counsel to lead a better life. She was dominated, certainly; but she was also endowed with a singular power by these men who feared her, who reassured themselves by proclaiming their native superiority at the top of their voice, but who believed her nevertheless to be capable of healing bodies and saving souls, and who entrusted themselves to women so that their mortal remains, after they had breathed their last, would be properly prepared, and their memory faithfully preserved for ever and ever.

Genealogies

These much simplified sketches are designed to help the reader among so many homonyms and to place the women discussed in this book.

Key: men △   women ○   marriage =   concubinage =/=

1 The Dukes of Normandy

Gisla = Rollo =/= *Poppa*
|
? = William Longsword =/= *Sprota*
|
Emma = Richard I =/= Gonnor
|
Richard II
|
Richard III   Robert =/= *Arlette*
|
William the Conqueror

2 The Counts of Guînes

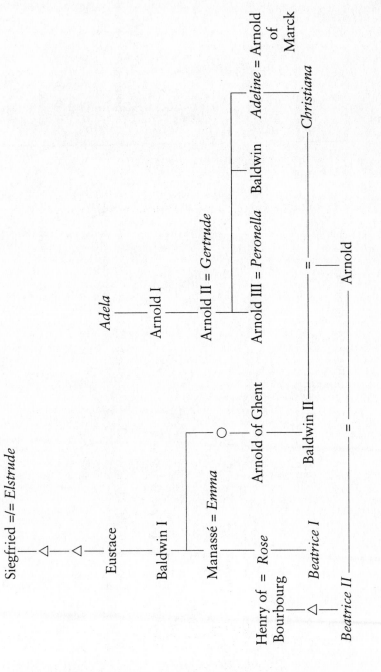

3 The Counts of Flanders

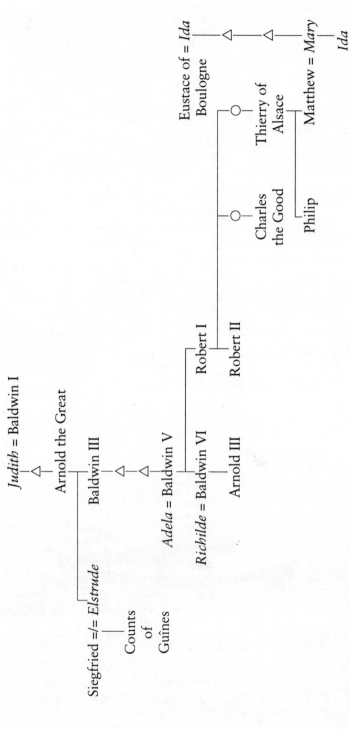